CHILDREN'S MINISTRY GUIDE TO USING DANCE AND DRAMA

Children's Ministry Guides

Children's Ministry has a commitment to provide the resources and training needed to help busy children's workers develop their ability to evangelize and disciple the children in their community.

Children's Ministry Guides are short, easy-to-read books offering practical insight into key areas of children's ministry. They complement the other resources and training opportunities available from Children's Ministry including

- conferences
- training days
- distance learning courses
- undated, activity-based, Bible-centred teaching programme
- books of ready-to-use ideas
- books of opinion and wisdom from children's ministry practitioners
- CDs and music books of children's praise songs
- supporting resources

For more details about the Children's Ministry range of resources visit www.childrensministry.co.uk or call 01323 437748.

Other titles in the series:

Using
Dance and Drama

RUTH ALLISTON
with
Jenny Brown, Cathy Kyte, Sue Price and Andy Back

Series edited by Sue Price

EASTBOURNE

ISBN 1 - 84291 - 092 - 2

Published by
KINGSWAY COMMUNICATIONS LTD,
Lottbridge Drove, Eastbourne, BN23 6NT, UK.
Cover design and print production for the publishers by
Bookprint Creative Services, P.O. Box 827, BN21 3YJ, England.
Printed in Great Britain.

To my father, who taught me that
the language of a cry expressed in multi-coloured,
multi-layered creativity will readily
open the door to God's heart.
Thank you, Papa.

Contents

Acknowledgments

I freely and gratefully acknowledge countless parents over many years who have generously entrusted their children to my care. What a privilege and delight it has been to explore together creative ways to love, honour and worship God, and to have our vision and expectation of him continually expanded. Thank you parents. Thank you children.

Introduction

The aim of this guide is to help you as you teach children about God and his rightful place in their lives. There are countless ways to do this, and dance and drama are just two of them. Tried and tested through the ages, and with new and changing forms, dance and drama form a valuable resource to bring children of the twenty-first century into a deeper knowledge and understanding of our great God. Dance and drama can be used to strengthen and intensify the relationship children have with God and each other.

It is not my intention to provide a global, comprehensive history of dance and drama through the ages, and you will find many gaps. Nor is it possible to list every idea or resource that you could use.

However, it is my hope that you will gain a wider understanding of the importance of dance and drama to God, enabling you to root them in him in the present day, in your location. Also, that from the ideas and examples given, you will be encouraged and inspired to create ones that will work well for the children you lead.

When pressed to describe dance, some people, with glazed eyes and a barely concealed yawn, mention ballet or ballroom dancing. To their fans, both these dance forms have much to admire and become excited about, but dance is about far more than these stylized examples. Human beings are dancers in a dancing universe. Dance is a foundational human activity, common to every tribe and culture worldwide, from earliest times. The desire to dance and move with rhythm develops in human beings before birth and through early infancy, as anyone will readily admit who has observed babies in utero and after birth, responding to music or rhythm.

If you still doubt the power and reality of rhythm and dance, look out for a local performance of the hit show, *Stomp*, that makes fascinating and compelling rhythm out of everything including the kitchen sink, or *Riverdance*. Dance and music are not just a physical product of limbs and instruments, but are a complete and mysterious combination of the whole body, mind and spirit that can offer worship, teach, express emotions, tell simple and profound stories, and bring colour and light to everyday events of life.

There are many reasons why you could have chosen to read this book. If your reason is not among those in the following short list, try to identify it now. Identifying your reason will enable you to pick out elements from the book that will serve you best.

- I'm already experienced in using dance and drama with groups of children and I'm looking for fresh motivation or ideas.

- I use dance (drama) with my group of children but have never tried drama (dance).
- I would like to use dance and drama but am not confident of my abilities or artistic qualities.
- I know nothing about either dance or drama but feel I ought to learn more.
- I've tried before to use dance and drama with children, but it hasn't worked out well.
- Someone has asked me to do some dance/drama with children. I feel under pressure and I don't know where to start.
- I'm desperate for new ideas and will try anything!
- Other reason?

Some may simply ask, Why should I use dance or drama with children in my group? This is a valid question, particularly for those of us who are not particularly interested in either medium. Part of the answer lies in the fact that dance and drama come from the heart of our creative God. They are already an integral part of our lives, but our awareness of their impact on us differs greatly from person to person. Dance and drama also have some very important practical, emotional, educational and spiritual benefits for those who choose to use them.

25 benefits of drama and dance

1. We express God's image within us through them.
2. They allow us to articulate thoughts, actions, feelings and emotions in a safe environment.
3. They can help us communicate with others.

4. Their skills and disciplines help promote self-control.
5. They can lift us beyond ourselves to God in worship.
6. They help us to learn more about God and ourselves.
7. They are fun.
8. They make learning a more interesting experience.
9. They help develop co-ordination skills.
10. They help develop concentration.
11. They can help us communicate with God.
12. They can have a therapeutic or cathartic effect, helping children tackle real-life issues in godly and constructive ways.
13. They can be used to teach right attitudes and responses to God and each other.
14. Especially when combined with music, as feelings are explored and displayed through characters, actions and emotions, they touch our spirits at a deeper level than many other learned crafts or skills.
15. They enable some children to excel, who may other wise find it difficult to express themselves or relate to others through writing, language or other skills and arts.
16. They improve our appreciation of the richness of language and music.
17. They develop imagination and artistic awareness.
18. They improve presentation skills and fluency of speech.
19. They are inclusive. No one need be excluded and they can help bond a group together.
20. They promote co-operation and working together.
21. They can involve parents and other adults, especially in productions.

22. They effect change in an invited audience by what they see, listen and learn of God.
23. They can provide welcome release or workout, especially for children who have limited exercise opportunities or freedom to play.
24. They can increase confidence.
25. They can provide opportunities for positive evaluation and praise.

1. God of dance

At creation, God the Holy Spirit hovered, fluttered, danced upon the waters that covered the dark, formless, empty earth. This hovering has rhythm, movement and sound and has been described as God's rhythmic presence. God's shadowing, hovering presence is expressed in several ways in the Bible.

Power to actively work to create change

In the dramatic song recited by Moses and recorded in Deuteronomy 32:10–11 he describes the actions of a mother eagle. When it's time to turn her young out of the nest, she rises up and hovers over the nest, stirring it up by the draught of her wings. She disrupts the nest, making it fall apart so that the eaglets will lose their safe, comfortable position and be forced out. She then stays, hovering, as they plummet and fall and test their wings. Her large, out-stretched wings are there to catch the eaglets if they fall beyond their ability to fly. This rhythmic hovering is one aspect of the work of the Holy Spirit, to move or change a situation; to be ready for action on God the Father's instructions.

Power to protect

God makes it plain through his Word that we are to value him as the source of all our joy, hope and fulfilment, instead of expecting him to value us as the source of his joy, hope and fulfilment. If we will cherish God in this way, we may take refuge under his wings and he will be present to give powerful protection for the sake of his glory, his Name. The shadowing presence of God's wings is not static, but moves and beats like the eagle's, dancing and soaring on the thermals. To know his protective, tangible, powerful, dancing presence that covers all, we too must be on the move constantly, imaging his movements, staying under those wings in God's current.

> He who dwells in the shelter of the Most High will rest in the shadow of the Almighty. I will say of the Lord, 'He is my refuge and my fortress, my God, in whom I trust.' Surely he will save you from the fowler's snare and from the deadly pestilence. He will cover you with his feathers, and under his wings you will find refuge. His faithfulness will be your shield and rampart. (Psalm 91:1–4)

> May the Lord repay you for what you have done. May you be richly rewarded by the Lord, the God of Israel, under whose wings you have come to take refuge.' (Ruth 2:12)

In creation, God introduced day and night, seasons, cycles, tides, planetary and magnetic forces, giving time and rhythm to his universe. These repetitive patterns give shape and harmony, as our universe moves, stirs, shifts and spins its dance through space. All this movement originates in God and although he does not have a physical body, these rhythms and patterns steadily beat like a great heart, pulsating strongly with love and power. They are never faltering, out of time or sync.

There is a rhythm or dance of language between created beings, both human and animal, to enable them to communicate with each other. Language is not just about learning to speak, read and write. Although initially some effort is required to learn a language, the best students learn quickest and easiest through entering into the rhythm and flow of the language. They may get some words wrong, but understanding is achieved because they have launched into the cadence and metre of the dance. Those who get bogged down in structure, grammar and spelling, though necessary at some point, lose the subtle movements of the dance steps of language.

The rhythm and dance of language works on a number of different levels from superficial to deeply intimate, but communication is about more than just spoken words. It also includes body language or non-verbal communication by which we give and receive information, and process it. Non-verbal communication in interpersonal relationships is a fascinating study, with patterns and dance steps, both universal and cultural, inborn and acquired. For those who believe in God, the Creator, this is yet another sign of his infinite care and attention to detail. The more we understand about language and communication, the more we appreciate the intricacy of its dance.

Non-verbal communication is articulated through facial expressions, body movement, sounds, tone of voice, eye contact and eye expression, personal space and dress. All of these convey a message in mostly silent dance steps so fast and fleeting as to be almost indiscernible. It is said that they account for three-quarters of our interpretation of what someone is 'saying'. Non-verbal communication supports the verbal messages we give. That is probably why text and e-mail messages often contain small constructed facial expressions to give life to words and help interpret them. However, there are times when our non-verbal communication is at odds with the words we say, making an extremely complicated dance.

Different people groups and tribes have some similarities of non-verbal communication, such as smiling, frowning or crying, but also some differences that seem odd to others and can lead to confusion and misunderstanding. For example, some of us find ourselves nodding in agreement as a friend talks. In some parts of the world, shaking the head is a sign of agreement.

The dance of language and communication is not just God's gift to human beings. God also created a dance of language and communication among animals, birds, insects, fish and reptiles. We are blessed to have so many nature and wildlife programmes and films to delight and teach us about God's creation, even though many of them try to exclude God from their subject. With each new discovery, patterns of dance and movement are uncovered. These too are often silent.

To watch birds, dolphins, whales and other creatures performing their body language and dance rituals is truly amazing. The complexities of communication and sensory perception between bees were first made public by an Austrian, Karl von Frish, one of the founders of the scientific study of animal behaviour. Building on the work of others, he demonstrated that bees communicate using body movements. Worker bees use complicated dances to convey information to their fellow bees. Von Frish wrote *The Dancing Room*, published in 1927. He revealed that on returning to the hive, foraging honeybees perform a figure of eight or round dance. The orientation and speed of the dances in relation to the sun and hive, combined with the waggling of the bee abdomen tell other worker bees preparing to leave the hive about the distance and direction of pollen or nectar sources.

God, who makes the beams of light that dance and flash upon water, must have dance at his heart. God who made the burning stars throb with his life and joy (Job 38:31-32) must delight in dance. Our God dances in the cloud shadows that cross a landscape, driven by the wind. He dances through fields of wheat and grass as the wind passes over them, and in the surf and waves of the sea.

God has set in motion everything we need for life, and sustains it all by his perpetual power and movement. God is not static, but ever moving on within the plans he's made, to see them fulfilled. We are born to the rhythm of the womb and God invites us to follow him into his dance. He stirs us on through life, into eternity with him. We cannot help but be drawn into the eternal dance of God, or deny a response to the rhythm that beats from his heart of love. We

are created to reflect that dance through our bodies, with
our emotions and spirits and feel its powerful expression
and communication. In this movement or dance, God is the
source, the destination, the choreographer and the means to
arrive. Just as Moses and the Hebrew people followed the
pillar of cloud by day and the dancing fire by night, so we
are constantly moving to follow our constantly moving
God. Through throbbing darkness and searing light, joy
and pain we follow, stirred with an elemental love that
comes from God himself to draw us ever after him.

2. Dance in Bible-times and the early church

God always intended that people should direct their worship to him as Creator with their whole spirits, minds and bodies. He wanted to have a constant and loving relationship with them under his care and direction, as he had with the first people in the Garden of Eden. From the time that Adam and Eve were evicted from the perfection of that state, God put his plan into action to restore that relationship and wholehearted worship from a people set apart for him alone. Other peoples gave their God-designed worship to false gods and things that God had created, but we can trace his desire, design and promise through the line of Noah, Abraham and Moses. In Scripture, God has allowed us to see his people's response and development as his chosen and called-out ones. Through succeeding generations we can observe and take comfort from their sometimes determined, sometimes faltering and imperfect steps, similar to our own, towards God, the true source and joy of life.

People in earlier times were much more comfortable with the universe than most of us are today, and more observant of the pace and natural rhythms of life. Among their earliest discoveries was the fact that shapes and patterns, movement, gesture and rhythm convey specific messages that cannot be expressed in any other way – primal communication. Dance for these people was not entertainment, but central to their existence. Dances were not performed for pleasure but were functional, serving a specific purpose and encompassing a huge variety of form, gesture, steps and silent language. For people with no knowledge of, or desire to know the one true God, Satan was able to corrupt God's beautiful gift of dance.

Functions of dance in communities

- Once the basic needs for food and shelter had been met, worship, thanksgiving or appeasement offered to gods or spirits of the dead was expressed through dance.
- Movement and dance celebrated the nature of the divinity and invoked their presence.
- Dance helped define areas of tribal belief e.g. the request for rain or the coming of the sun.
- A spiritual link was created by dance between deity and people whereby good or evil spirits were summoned for health, fertility and curing of illness, or for retribution, infertility and death.
- Dance was used to offer sacrifice, a body for possession, or purification.
- Pleas to avert calamity or invite prosperity were offered through dance.

- The monotony of everyday routines, such as pounding or threshing grain, was relieved by rhythm and dance.
- Dance provided a natural means for expressing emotions of joy, sadness and fear.
- A sense of corporate belonging and the telling of tribal stories were effected through dance.
- Dance defined the social identity of the group, male and female, marking progress of individuals from birth to death through initiation, ceremonies and rites.
- Crop cycles and tribal events were celebrated through dance.
- Dance heralded preparations for war, and celebrated victory or signalled defeat.
- It created communication between dancers and released tensions.
- It encouraged discipline in people and and gave shape to their lives.

Amid temptations to give their love and allegiance to false gods, God's people were called to reflect and celebrate a covenant heart-to-heart relationship of love and deep commitment with the true and living God. This was to be expressed by faith in him alone, obedience to his laws and ways and trust in his eternal goodness.

The Hebrew word *hésed* is not easily translated into English, but carries the meaning of steadfast love and faithfulness, binding two parties in joyful willingness. God's poetic, heartfelt word to his people through Hosea the prophet showed his pain that they could so easily cast aside their covenant. No broken legal obligation only, but a deep betrayal of loyalty and relationship.

Bible-times dances of God's people are set in this context, as they responded joyfully to his will and purposes for them. In middle-eastern cultures ring dances in particular were used to circle altars and worship gods. The sinfully defiant dance around the golden calf was a pagan worship ring dance reflecting the ancient Egyptian cult of Apis, the bull god (Exodus 32). When Elijah challenged the priests to call on Baal, known as Lord of the dance, to make fire on the altar at Mount Carmel, they leapt themselves into exhaustion in an ecstatic ring dance (1 Kings 18).

This verse is another example of the ring dance, the circling of the altar in the temple, used by God's people to worship him.

> I wash my hands in innocence, and go about (encompass) your altar, O Lord, proclaiming aloud your praise and telling of all your wonderful deeds. I love the house where you live, O Lord, the place where your glory dwells. (Psalm 26:6)

Four of the five Hebrew words for dance are connected with religious activities and worship of God, and people, priests and prophets danced before him in thanksgiving, worship, celebration and victory.

> When the men were returning home after David had killed the Philistine, the women came out from all the towns of Israel to meet King Saul with singing and dancing, with joyful songs and with tambourines and lutes. (1 Samuel 18:6)

> Let Israel rejoice in their Maker; let the people of Zion be glad in their King. Let them praise his name with dancing and make

music to him with tambourine and harp. For the Lord takes delight in his people; he crowns the humble with salvation. (Psalm 149:3)

A processional dance was used by King David when king, priests and people accompanied the Ark of the Covenant. God was present in the Ark, and they danced in his presence.

Now David was clothed in a robe of fine linen, as were all the Levites who were carrying the ark, and as were the singers, and Kenaniah, who was in charge of the singing of the choirs. David also wore a linen ephod. So all Israel brought up the ark of the covenant of the Lord with shouts, with the sounding of rams' horns and trumpets and of cymbals, and the playing of lyres and harps. As the ark of the covenant of the Lord was entering the City of David, Michal, daughter of Saul watched from a window.

(1 Chronicles 15:27–29)

It was common practice for prophets to experience the presence of their gods through intense ecstatic dance. It seems to have been an acceptable practice for God's prophets too.

In Old Testament times there were companies of prophets, or religious communities, who banded together for mutual support and cultivation of their zeal for God through this form of dance, associated with prophecy (Numbers 11:25–27; 1 Samuel 10:5–7; 1 Samuel 19:18–24).

There is no specific mention of dance in the New Testament as a form of worship offered to God as the Christian church came into being, and people joyfully accepted Jesus as Lord. Although in one sense everything had changed, yet God remained the same and the need to express a loving, thankful response to him remained the same.

The Holy Spirit is a Spirit of joy. Paul cautioned Christians at Ephesus to be filled with the Spirit rather than wine (Ephesians 5:18–19), inferring that just as some people find joy and release in wine, Christians can enjoy God in liberation and spontaneity by singing and making music, with thanksgiving.

It's hard to believe that New Testament worship did not include the same physical expression of dance as God's people had enjoyed in Old Testament times. Paul's instructions on orderly worship (1 Corinthians 14:26–40) addressed specific issues in the Corinthian church and were not intended to repress the expression of Holy Spirit joy.

It would seem that early Christians accepted dance as an integral part of worship, following the pattern of earlier Bible times. Clement of Alexandria, a Christian theologian (AD150–216), is quoted as saying: 'Then shalt thou dance in a ring, together with the angels, round Him who is without beginning nor end, the only true God, and God's Word is part of our song.'

The ring dance, processional dance, individual prophetic and worship dance are just a few of the different forms that continued to be used in worship throughout the following centuries. They enabled people to participate in the divine mysteries that surround God, express great joy and articulate belief and faith in our living God.

Throughout Christian history, Christians who wished to dance had the Word of God as their ultimate sanction, his joy in their spirits and his Holy Spirit energy in their bodies and feet. And so it remains today. Christians – including children - across the world who experience greater freedom of worship, more knowledge and understanding of the truth than our forebears, and who know the hope to which they are called, can celebrate and dance before God with all that they have and are. This includes the use of musical instruments, shouts of praise, processions, prophetic singing and dance, along with King David, the angels and the courts of heaven, saints from the past, brothers and sisters everywhere. An unbroken, eternal ring of dance around God's throne.

3. Using dance with under 5s

Most small children have no problem moving around. Indeed, most find it hard to be still!

For our purposes, dance has several aims, which may stand alone, or combine with each other:

- Dance can aid the telling of a story, or drama.
- Dance can safely dissipate energy, feelings and emotions.
- Dance can be fun and enjoyed for itself alone.
- Dance can be one expression of praise or worship and direct children's limited and immature understanding of God to its source.

While some children may be well co-ordinated and naturally rhythmic, purists would not call most of what small children do, dance.

However smooth or faltering, their attempts express something of what they think and feel, their enjoyment of the moment, or their desire to worship God. These touch his heart and he swiftly responds with his total acceptance, love and approval. And that's all that matters.

Dance can be spontaneous and instinctive

Parents and leaders will be familiar with this type of dance. Joy, excitement and pleasure, and sometimes anger and sadness, can cause small children to break into movement and dance without thinking about it. Make opportunity for these moments in your programme. Your meeting space should already be as safe and child-friendly as possible. Train helpers to be ready and child-aware so children can enjoy the freedom of movement and dance. It isn't necessary to direct children's responses, only to make sure they are safe. Encourage children by example to respond in their own way to thoughts, feelings and emotions generated by the stories, songs, rhymes, games, fun, praise and ideas included in your programme. Such ways might include jumping up and down, spinning round alone or with a partner, jigging, hopping, skipping, prancing or galloping, flying or running round. Young children can't process abstract thoughts and feelings and will need to anchor them in a person or a situation. Don't conclude spontaneous dance with negative feelings or emotions. Always finish positively.

Don't be limited by your meeting space. Although we want children to be spontaneous in their responses, some planning can spark off very special and individual experiences within a group. For all activities where extra help is needed, follow your church policy for recruiting adults.

• Are there deciduous trees near where you meet? How can you safely make opportunity for children to run, jump, roll and dance through drifts of crunchy autumn leaves? If necessary, import bags of dried leaves indoors. Afterwards, provide brooms, dustpans and brushes for children to enjoy sweeping them up. The sounds and scent of the leaves add another heady dimension to the experience and can be used to lead into thanksgiving and praise of God.

- Be ready in winter in case it should snow. Suitably dressed, children can jump and catch snowflakes, and dance like them, giving opportunity to marvel at God's creation. Look for songs and poems to use indoors afterwards about snow, and together discover actions for them.

- What about rain and puddles? If you know it's going to rain when you meet, telephone parents and ask them to bring children appropriately dressed, with boots. Of course it takes time and effort to dress everyone, prime enough helpers and get children dried and sorted afterwards, but the obvious joy of jumping, splashing and dancing through puddles, alone or as Follow my Leader, is a rare treat for everyone.

- Arrange a bedtime blessing. Talk to parents about a special treat one dark winter's evening. Fix a time when you can be fairly sure of having a clear sky. If children are allowed to stay up a little longer than usual it will add to the excitement. Meet at a local hill or high spot away from street lights. Take warm drinks, blankets to wrap everyone in and a CD player. Look at the stars together. Let children jump to try and touch them. Create a circle dance to *God made the stars*, and *Praise him, praise him* from 'Thank you God for Snails' CD. Make a praise shout together with a sentence from Psalm 148:3-4. Finish with a song and dance, *God is good* from the same CD. Make the time short, but meaningful. Thank God for his greatness and his love for the children and their families. This activity can be followed up another time with a collage frieze of stars, displaying children's comments, thoughts and ideas about God's creation of stars.

- Do you live near enough to the sea to arrange a beach picnic? With plenty of practical adult help, provide shade, sunscreen, first aid kit and make sure everyone has a hat. Small children can be frightened by the hugeness of the sea and won't all want to paddle or touch seaweed. Dig a pool further back from the edge and encourage children to dip their toes in. Investigate sand and sea creatures and rock pools. Dig holes and castles. Watch and interpret the different kinds of dancing waves and the seagulls. Collect shells or stones. Bring back small treasures to display for children later as a discussion point for thanking God or use them to illustrate a story of Jesus at the seaside. Of course, children must be watched and accounted for all the time, but this need not prevent the pleasures of the seaside and fresh air. Make up a dance to the song, *Oh I do like to be beside the seaside*, for children to march, play and dance on the sand with bare feet.

Dance can spring from an idea and be improvised

- Rhyme is a dance of words and a very natural and useful tool to implant thoughts, ideas and whole stories into children's minds and hearts. Rhymes should contain simple words that are part of children's vocabulary and can be either spoken or sung to familiar tunes e.g. nursery rhymes and songs.

EXAMPLE: ISAAC IS BORN

Genesis 18:1–15: 21:1–7.
Tune – London Bridge is falling down.
God is good all the time,
All the time, all the time.
God is good all the time;
All the time.
Say the rhyme aloud slowly and expressively several times for children to hear all the words and rhythm. Put the rhyme, music and dance together and repeat several times.

- Clapping or stamping out the rhythm can be a helpful introduction to movement. The ability to speak or sing with dance or actions simultaneously develops as children grow. Younger children will probably not be able to do both at once, and the rhyme needs to be supported by adults to allow children freedom to move or dance. Young children have a tendency to pick up strange ideas even when we think we've spoken clearly. Two or three brief questions can check children's understanding of the story, idea to be expressed or the feelings experienced. Encourage children to think of dance actions for those ideas. They don't have to be same as each other's actions. What kind of dance can we do …
  … when we sing about God?
  … to show what 'good' means?
  … to show time?
- Check out your CD collection and list excerpts of music

that convey different moods and feelings to fit different themes and stories e.g. sad, happy, busy, gentle, fighting or being cross, tired etc. Children of this age are not critical of your music tastes and have few hang-ups over classical, hillbilly or reggae. Don't limit yourself or the children by your choices. Play your selected music for children to hear. What does this make you think of? Encourage children to dance out their answer to the music, and join in.

- When playing music or singing songs, or looking for accompaniment to a story, provide ribbon or crepe paper streamers for children to wave. Ribbons can be attached to elastic to fit over a child's hand or finger. Make sure they have enough space to wave freely without endangering others. If possible give children a choice of colours, relating their choice to a character, feeling or story component e.g. What colour streamer will you choose for Mary? What colour is being cross? What colour is fire? Assure them it's fine to have a different choice from others. Sometimes children can be encouraged, in groups, to form a stream of moving colour to represent the sea, wind, clouds, fire, trees, etc.

- Look out for cheap material. Markets and Asian shops are very reasonable sources of wonderful colours and textures such as Chinese Silk. Four metres of material is a good length for a group of children and helpers to hold, roll, ripple, lift and let fall while others take turns to run or dance underneath. You can use different colours to represent different effects e.g. green, blue, turquoise for water, seas and rivers. These can be held by helpers at each end and rippled across the floor for children to jump, roll and dance in. Red, orange and yellow can be used for flames of fire. White and grey can be used for rain and mountains. Gold, silver and purple can be used for God and his glory.

- Invest in a good quality bubble blower and bubble liquid e.g. Early Learning Centre. Bubbles can be used very effectively on occasions to encourage children to dance, clap and stamp.

Dance can be directed or choreographed

Small children have short concentration spans. Keep dance activities brief, with simple instructions. If you wish to repeat an activity several times but children have already lost interest, leave it and try again later in your programme.

- Action rhymes and songs with pre-scripted actions can easily be taught to small children. These are often a good way to help shy children move more freely. Know your children well. Some may feel more confident if they are able to copy others who are doing the same actions, rather than have to think of their own. Give them the opportunity to relax and enjoy moving, and with plenty of encouragement, they may well move on to dance more spontaneously.

EXAMPLE: GOD MADE PEOPLE

Genesis 1:26–31; 2:18–22.
Say the rhyme with actions, and repeat for children to copy the actions.
I can't be an elephant, or a kangaroo.

Use an arm for an elephant trunk, jump like a kangaroo
I can't be the cow with the loudest, 'Moo.'
'Moo ' loudly.
I can't be a tree waving in the breeze.
Wave arms like branches.
I can't be the plants that live under the seas.
Crouch down, waving hands gently.
I can only be the child that you see.
Stand up straight.
I'm the special person God made me to be.
Jump and clap hands above head.

- Look for music and songs with actions on the theme of your choice that will encourage children into movement and dance e.g. *If I were a Butterfly* or *God made my hands* from 'Children's Praise and Worship for under 5s' CD, or *On my tiptoes I am tall* from 'Ishmael's Little Songs for Little Children' CD. Small bells threaded onto shirring elastic and worn around wrists or ankles can encourage children to move more freely.

- Learning to work and play with others is a developmental ability. Some children in your group may not yet be able to do this and still work and play alongside others, rather than with them. This can affect any dance projects you plan for children in pairs or small groups. Again, know your children well and prepare your dance plans accordingly. One way of overcoming this is to use a group circle with pre-thought-out dance actions for your theme or story, or a dance line. The dance line is formed with a leader at its head, and helpers interspersed between children. The simplest dance line has everyone holding hands and following the leader around your meeting space, copying the steps of leader and helpers. Once children understand how the dance line works and enjoy it, they can let go of hands and still follow the leader, copying a wider range of dance actions.

- Look at your story or theme from a dance viewpoint. Work out simple dance movements for actions in the story. Enlist the help of a keyboard player and work out a series of sounds for these movements. Play them to children and practise the brief dances together. These can be incorporated into your story or theme e.g. falling rain, flowers opening, trees rustling, soldiers marching, angels appearing, night-time, stormy weather, etc.

4. Using dance with 5-9s

The age groups used in this book have fuzzy edges and you may find that some younger children in the five to nine years range will benefit from ideas used with under-fives, and older children may benefit from ideas suggested for over nines.

The purpose of using dance with children in this age group has similar aims to those for younger children:

- Dance can aid the telling of a story, or drama, making it more memorable.
- Dance can be a painless vehicle for a teaching point.
- Dance can safely and creatively dissipate energy, feelings and emotions.
- Dance can be fun and enjoyed for itself alone.
- Dance can be one expression of praise or worship and direct children's limited, but growing, understanding of God to its source.

Child development experts tell us that children learn best through active involvement, and dance in its varied forms is a perfect vehicle for this. Although young children have many questions that tax parents and leaders alike, up to around seven years old children generally accept and believe the answers given. Abstract thought and the ability to think more broadly or hypothetically only develops after about twelve years of age. The ages from five to nine are ideal years in which to teach biblical and life truths and to develop children's relationship with God.

Dance with children can combine their love of being busy and active with learning, and can also encourage their need to be, to wonder, to reflect and process information and ideas. Many children lead rushed and very full lives. Dance can help smooth their way forward and provide opportunities and oases of thinking and creative space.

Boys may culturally have a more limited understanding of the breadth and scope of dance activities and will need to see dance presented in ways that motivate them to want to take part. Marie Bensley, who operates dance workshops with Kingdom Dance, says that boys may be put off by even the word 'dance' and recommends calling it 'High Energy Praise.' Whatever term you choose to use, both boys and girls will benefit from as wide a range of dance activities that your creativity can devise. Whether you feel you have the creativity or skills or not to promote dance, it's always worth seeking out others to contribute ideas, enthusiasm and practical help. Build a team or pool of human resources who are divinely inspired.

Get to know the children's interests and things they enjoy doing. Use these as a basis for your team to work on for ideas. Be prepared to put aside your own preferences for particular forms of dance and begin from where children are. When they are enjoying dance in a form acceptable to them you may be able to gradually widen their horizons and introduce other shapes and structures of dance.

If you have worked with your group of children for any length of time you will know that however creative or helpful your ideas for children's learning, enjoyment, growth and spiritual development, these work best within a framework of discipline, springing from genuine, loving care. In this context you and your team will need to consistently teach children that listening to and obeying instructions is important so that everyone can enjoy the dance experience. Any props used for dance are only to be used for that purpose. They are not weapons or toys. Dance props should only be given out when you are ready to begin, and should be collected afterwards and put away. This will not only help to stop their abuse, but also ensure that children don't become bored with them by easy access.

Dance or rhythmic movement is most often used as an accompaniment or visual expression of a story told through music, song, drama, narration, choral speaking, story or spoken rhyme. Dance and rhythm combined with music and drama/spoken word has the potential to involve all children. These don't need to be complicated productions. Simple arrangements on your theme or story can sometimes be the most effective.

1. Choose your theme, teaching point or story.
2. Decide the style you will use to carry the words e.g. song, drama, narration, choral speaking, story or spoken rhyme.

3. With your team, work out the script line by line and write it out.
4. Find the right music to accompany it.
5. Work out the rhythm or dance steps and write them out.
6. Find the props you need for the dance, if required.
7. Practise the dance and script with your team.
8. If possible, demonstrate it to children then invite them to join in as you repeat it.

You may not immediately think of some of the following forms of rhythmic movement as dance, and you may well be right. However, they have an important place and serve as an enjoyable introduction to dance in its more recognizable forms.

• Spoken rhyme with song.

EXAMPLE: GOD'S PEOPLE PRAY TOGETHER

2 Chronicles 20:1–30.

This Bible story tells of a time when God's people heard that their enemies were almost at the city gate. In their fear and panic they prayed together to God. He heard their prayer and answered in a surprising and powerful way.

Line everyone up at one end of your space. Link arms to form a tight line. Show how to march in step, starting with the left foot. Left, right. Left, right, still keeping the tight line. March across the space together. Turn and march back, this time marching and singing or chanting.

The more we are together, together, together,
The more we are together, the stronger we will be.
I'm strong, and you're strong.

We're strong, we're all strong.
The more we are together, the stronger we will be.

- Most children enjoy using flags. These are simply made from material and dowelling. Timber merchants will cut dowelling to the length you need. The handle end of the pole is best kept short. The ends of each length can be smoothed with glasspaper. Look for bright jewel colours and glittery materials in markets and Asian shops. Find a friend with a sewing machine. Flags can be made in different sizes. The larger the flag, the more space, practice and control they need. To begin, make sure you have a large space for children to be safe. Find a couple of songs that children know e.g. *Colours of salvation* from Jim Bailey's 'All over Again' CD. Talk about the words and meanings and encourage them to think of movements and interpretation with the flags. You can designate different colours for different effects e.g. love of God, fire of God, Holy Spirit, prayer for others, forgiveness, asking help, worship, thanksgiving, praise, etc. Processions and counter-marching with music and song are also effective with flags.
- As with three to five-year-olds, lengths of material and ribbon or crepe paper streamers are very acceptable ways of introducing movement and dance to music and story-telling. Older children can be more adventurous with streamers, making figure of eight actions and body-swirling.
- Counter-marching to spoken rhyme can also be an energetic form of rhythmic movement. Begin by teaching the words and rhythm. Children can stamp out the rhythm

while saying the words. Make two groups to stand in a well-spaced line at either end of the room. Children should be facing a gap in the opposite group, not a child. Practise left, right marching on the spot. At a given signal begin the rhyme and each line moves forward, keeping in step and line horizontally, passing between other children on the way. Depending on the length of the rhyme and the size of the room, children can turn and return to the starting point.

- Rap is a popular form of spoken rhythm, sometimes half-sung. Familiarize yourself with children's rap music. Encourage children to help you write a rap on your chosen topic or story. They can work out their movements, using the rhythm and the story as their guide.
- Stick-dancing to music or rhyme can be used effectively. Ask a timber merchant to cut lengths of dowelling 3cms x 60cms, one per child. Smooth the ends with glasspaper. Work out with your team a set of dance and rhythm movements for small groups of well-supervised children, combining stamping feet, stamping the stick on the floor, clashing sticks together.
- Occasionally some children might like to use rhythm or percussion instruments while others dance. Practise the rhythm together and encourage children to keep time by watching a leader who conducts or beats time.
- The simplest actions can evolve into dance of sorts.

EXAMPLE: JESUS TEACHES ABOUT FORGIVENESS

Matthew 18:21–35.
Write out the words of the song. Mark a start and finish line.

Teach the song to the tune, *Old Macdonald had a farm.*
Over and over and over and over,
Over and over again.
How many times should we forgive?
Over and over again.
Forgive here, forgive there,
Here, there, here, there,
Here, there, and more to spare.
How many times should we forgive?
Over and over again.
Have children crouch down on the start line. They can make roly-poly somersaults all the way to the finish line and back again, while trying to sing the song at the same time.

- Before starting a song that will lead into praise or worship of God, encourage children to be ready to dance for God. Pray for them. Play the song and give practical instruction, demonstrating the kind of movements the song inspires. Ask children for their ideas and be ready to set an example with your helpers. Don't push children into dancing if they don't want to. If they are uncomfortable when others are dancing, give them opportunity to join in the rhythm with instruments, jumping, clapping, clicking fingers, whistling, etc.
- Hoops can be a useful tool for pair, group or circle dancing especially, but not exclusively, for girls. Use material and silk or plastic flowers, or crepe paper. Children can choose a colour theme and help make them. Bind strips of material or crepe paper around the hoops to cover the plastic. Make paper flowers and fix these (or the silk

flowers) firmly with sticky tape at intervals around the hoops.

5. Using dance with over 9s

Many of the points in the chapter on using drama with over nines apply to using dance with children of this age.

You may have the perfect group of children who are growing and going on with God and who regularly enjoy dance as part of their worship of him, with huge amounts of delight and gusto. However, if you feel that your journey towards perfection, or heaven, has scarcely begun, take heart!

It's always sad for parents and leaders to see children who once moved so freely, and worshipped God easily and gladly, gradually slip into what appears to be apathy, embarrassment and a tangle of unco-ordinated limbs. It doesn't happen for all children, but if this describes some of the children in your group, don't give up on them, and don't panic or despair. It may have more to do with peer pressure and growing outside interests than backsliding. However, do pray consistently for each child, lifting them to God and asking that what has already been sown in their minds and hearts will grow strong and true, with both blossom and fruit for God. Don't allow doubts or disappointments to cloud your picture of that child or children, worshipping God freely. Many, many children and adults have been won for God through persistent prayer of parents, leaders and helpers. Your prayers are one of the most important and life-changing things you can do for those in your group.

Picture your group now, the place you meet and how it's set up. Do children sit slumped around a table, carefully contained? This may be helpful to you, but it's unlikely to motivate or liberate children to want to dance. Aim to create a context of moving freely within the group throughout your time together with games, quizzes, activities, music and drama. Look carefully at your programme to discover safe, fun and comfortable ways to generate more movement.

- Food and drink are always helpful. Arrange a rota of reliable cakemakers or snack providers, taking care to provide suitable fare for those with food allergies. Make several snackstops between activities for children to move around and serve themselves.
- Celebrate birthdays or achievements (however small) with party poppers, large graffiti wall and marker pens for messages and pictures, kazoos, songs, applause, stamping and whistling, etc. This not only provides freedom of movement, but also helps children positively affirm each other within the peer group.

The purpose of movement is to encourage children to move unself-consciously and in natural ways. It is not natural for children to sit still, and they will be extremely self-conscious if then asked to leap around to worship God. It also gives an unhelpful message as to what pleases God and passes for worship. Of course it's necessary to maintain discipline. Set out ground rules for acceptable behaviour and review them regularly with children so they know the standard required.

Even discussion needs sometimes to be loosed from the confines of sitting, into more active ways of producing new ideas or conveying truth. Apply some lateral thinking to the topic for discussion.

EXAMPLE: FRIENDSHIP

Have someone draw round a friend on paper and place the picture at the far end of the room. As ideas for what makes a good friend are generated, children can draw or write them out and go and stick them on the picture. Children can write the names of their friends, or draw them, and stick them on, too. Comparisons and assessments can be made of current friendships. Finally, children can write their own names and stick them on, deciding what kind of friend they are.

Of course, constant, frenetic activity is not what's required. There must be a balance, with time for chilling out and relaxation. During quieter spaces in your programme when children might be thinking or working on their own, or in smaller groups, play music. Adults might prefer background music for this kind of activity, but children prefer it louder and some may respond with tapping, or other movement.

• Some of the ideas used with five to nine-year-olds can be

used successfully in slightly different forms for older children. Encourage cross-movement between groups, teaching older children the principles of being a role model and how to actively join in. They will probably be less self-conscious with younger children, and even enjoy the experience.

- Find out, and keep up-to-date, with the different kinds of music children enjoy. Research CDs by Christian artists and bands in these styles and play some tracks for children to hear e.g. *Kindle* by Screaming Serenades, *Unashamed* by Paul Oakley. Older children might be interested to look through a magazine with you such as *Juice* that has reviews of music releases from rock to classical, hip-hop to praise and worship. Talk about why we dance in response to music, and where. Why do people dance for God, how and where? Listen carefully to children's answers. If you have enough children to make a small group for several different styles of music, they can each choose a song and work out a style of dance to fit it. These can be performed in turn for the whole group.

- Regularly read Christian magazines and networks to find out if there are concerts, praise parties, camps, summer schools, etc. anywhere near you for children in this age group. Children sometimes find it easier to join in praise and worship in a large group setting. Take the opportunity to talk through all the issues involved and encourage children to be ready for God to energize and liberate them.

- Are any of the children in your group breakdance experts? If so, encourage it. If they are able to teach others, let them. Otherwise, search out a godly role model who can teach children this form of dance as an offering to God. Help children research musical accompaniment if required. When recruiting regular or extra adult helpers, follow your church policy.

• Rap is a very useful tool for children of this age. They are more able to write their own words on a theme, Bible verse or story or psalm, and activate its rhythm. Rap takes practice and persistence, but is well worth the effort.

EXAMPLE: JONAH RAP

Listen up in the house, got a message for you
About a sea creature who had something to spew;
I was just lying there on my towel on the sand
When this great fish vomited on the dry land:
Did a technicolour yawn (and there was lots of it –
Diced carrots and seaweed and a runaway prophet).

• When using drama, explore with children possibilities of adding dimensions of dance or rhythm.
• As children become more used to dance, some of them may enjoy listening to an excerpt from a piece of music, or a song, and interpreting a solo or group dance to what they hear.
• If children are not interested in dance, think about other forms of movement that could be offered to God. It's important to know or find out activities children enjoy and work out together how these can be used as dance forms. These will not be considered formal or normal dance by children or anyone else. However, offered to

God in a spirit of joy, thanksgiving, praise or worship, participants find that he is not picky and will enjoy it with them! Some children are not as active as others, or feel embarrassed about moving around. You will need Holy Spirit inspiration to discover new dance forms with them. You may need to change your meeting place, arrange other times and places for children to meet for this purpose, or find ways to incorporate them into your meeting. Any of the following ideas, and more that children will think of, can be used for this purpose:

1. Many children enjoy using their bikes to display amazing feats of balance and daring. They spend hours on bike pads, spare ground or anywhere they are allowed, creating, copying and practising.

2. Skateboarders have a similar passion for action, movement and display. Find out what local skate parks or pads you have.

3. Rollerbladers, fast-moving and agile, jumping, weaving and ducking, enjoy their freedom and expertise.

4. The old hobby of kite flying has been transformed with new and wondrous kites that thrill, and challenge coordination.

5. Ball skills in football can be used with music or rhyme to create dance.

6. Some girls might prefer praise aerobics. There are specific videos on this topic or with help, they could create their own. Gymnastics is another option. You will need to find older children, teens or adults who are experienced in these 'dance' activities, preferably those who are going on with God and who can become excellent role models for those in your group. Encourage them to work with

children on their particular interest and to discover ways
to offer it to God. A portable CD player and CDs chosen
by children can turn their activity into a dance for God,
even if they never call it by that name. Challenge them to
find a name for it. For all activities, safety is paramount,
and protective gear must be worn where necessary. You
will also need plenty of adult supervision apart from
'experts.'

7. Some children may enjoy the simple pleasure of running
   or rolling down a steep hill. What about grass toboggan-
   ing combined with praise shouts? Challenge children to
   think how such activities can be used to praise God.

8. Do you have children interested in more formal sports or
   athletics? Make enquiries about Christians in Sport and
   find role models for children. How can their chosen
   sport, as part of their life, be offered to God as worship?
   Watch the video *Chariots of Fire* and discuss Eric Liddell's
   statement, 'When I run, I feel God's pleasure.'

You may feel overwhelmed by the thought of setting up
some of these activities or altering the way your group
operates. One of the functions of the Holy Spirit is to pro-
voke and stimulate. Allow him to do his work in your mind
and heart, and prepare to have your thinking changed if
necessary on the whole subject of dance.

Our desire is for children to find freedom to express to
God their thanksgiving for the joys of life and his great love
for them, and to be able to return that love. For children,
this freedom of expression finds its outlet in physical ways
that are natural to them, and that are an extension of their
own lives and being. They will need our help to discover

these ways, but they must own and enjoy them. We live in times where increasingly children are not free to enjoy and display these elemental responses. Fears and precautions for their safety, sedentary and solitary pastimes, peer pressure, worldly influences, school and exam pressures, and worries about relationships, easily drain the joy from life and leave children the poorer.

Oh, that they might dance their way into God's heart, and stay there!

6. God of drama

God's acts, both in creation and his continuing, unfolding revelation of his being and plans have been, and continue to be, played upon the stage of time and history. We could not know our Designer, Creator, Director, Producer, Stage Manager, unless he revealed himself to us. He has drawn back the curtain covering the stage and allowed us to see the universal drama of his plan of salvation for mankind. With awe and anticipation we can look backwards and forwards through his production. God has allowed us to know the outline story from beginning to end, even though there are many gaps to be filled and events to be coloured. We can watch this breathtaking, cosmic drama unfold, with the greatest designer, director and producer ever known. As we both watch, and take part, God gives ever-deepening insights into his love and wisdom, with each succeeding generation.

Have you ever watched a lavish stage production such as *The Lion King*? This huge, magical mix of fantasy and reality is woven together by the creativity, energy and stage-craft of writers, composers, musicians, costume designers, lighting engineers, choreographers, dancers, acrobats, ath-letes, poets, technical support, sound engineers and many other artistic components. We can admire and appreciate such productions with breath-held wonder, but these are as shadows compared with the drama created and produced by God.

Nature is the divine display of God's handiwork in cre-ation. Read Job 38–39 and Psalm 104 to catch glimpses of God's dramatic power through his creation. The graphic word pictures form a thrilling stage show in our minds that leads us to praise God and bow down in worship. God's beautiful world forms a backdrop to his drama that sur-passes anything we could ever conceive.

God doesn't just produce and direct his drama from the wings, or leave the characters he has created to improvise their own stage play. From the very beginning of Act 1, he appears and speaks personally on his own stage to his cast, intervening and directing, read Genesis 3:8–19; 9:1–17.

All the way through time God continues to appear, to encourage and manage those he has chosen in dramatic ways.

The Lord said, 'Go out and stand on the mountain in the presence of the Lord, for the Lord is about to pass by.' Then a great and powerful wind tore the mountains apart and shattered the rocks before the Lord, but the Lord was not in the wind. After the wind there was an earthquake, but the Lord was not in the earthquake. After the earthquake came a fire, but the Lord was not in the fire. And after the fire came a gentle whisper.' (1 Kings 19:11–12)

For the eyes of the Lord range throughout the earth to strengthen
those whose hearts are fully committed to him.

(2 Chronicles 16:9)

The Lord told him, 'Go to the house of Judas on Straight Street,
and ask for a man from Tarsus named Saul, for he is praying. In a
vision he has seen a man named Ananias come and place his
hands on him to restore his sight.' (Acts 9:11–12)

Think of books you have read recently that tell how God
spoke directly into someone's life drama. What about your
own life drama? How is God currently appearing, or
encouraging, intervening and directing your story?

And on into Act 2: eternity, God continues to appear,
speak and direct.

And I heard a loud voice from the throne saying, 'Now the
dwelling of God is with men, and he will live with them. They will
be his people, and God himself will be with them and he their
God. He will wipe every tear from their eyes. There will be no
more death or mourning or crying or pain, for the old order of
things has passed away.' He who was seated on the throne said, 'I
am making everything new!' Then he said, 'Write this down, for
these words are trustworthy and true.' He said to me: 'It is done.
I am the Alpha and the Omega, the Beginning and the End. To him
who is thirsty I will give to drink without cost from the water of
life. He who overcomes will inherit all this, and I will be his God
and he will be my son.' (Revelation 21.1–7)

God's Word is not just spoken word, dramatic as this is, but
the Hebrew image of 'word' (*dabar*) carries the meaning of

an event and action, and God-breathed dynamic purpose. This Hebrew concept was grasped and understood by Bible-times people.

> And God said, 'Let there be light,' and there was light.
>
> (Genesis 1:3)

> As the rain and the snow come down from heaven, and do not return to it without watering the earth and making it bud and flourish, so that it yields seed for the sower and bread for the eater, so is my word that goes out from my mouth: it will not return to me empty, but will accomplish what I desire and achieve the purpose for which I sent it. (Isaiah 55:10–11)

> In the beginning was the Word, and the Word was with God, and the Word was God. He was with God in the beginning. Through him all things were made; without him nothing was made that has been made. In him was life, and that life was the light of men.... The Word became flesh and made his dwelling among us. We have seen his glory, the glory of the One and Only, who came from the Father, full of grace and truth. (John 1:1–4; 14)

God inspired the writer of Genesis with information and events known only to God. Although these are written concisely, they begin a great historical drama from God's point of view. Prose describes the beginnings of the universe and the creation of life in Genesis 1. However, in verse 27 God suddenly breaks into poetry – the language of feeling and emotion - when speaking about the creation of people, male and female.

Other things God made gave him great pleasure, but

human beings were radically different from everything else he made. These special creatures were formed to bring glory to his Name. That these would be the ones who would eventually lead the whole of creation to worship his beautiful Son, Jesus, captured God's heart, and poetry burst out. God breathed his life into us, and we inhaled it.

Genesis sets the stage, gives the cast and the plot of the whole drama of redemption. It sets out questions that cry out for answers: What's gone wrong with the world? How can it be put right? Where did we come from? Why do we have to die? God answers these questions through the drama of people's lives set out in the Bible.

God designed and made us tripartite - spirit, mind and body. We are created to respond freely to God, his life and work within us, with every part of us. Tripartite beings, we are to reflect the glory of our triune God, displaying his multicoloured, manifest wisdom and beauty throughout the whole of time and history and on into eternity.

We each have a part to play in God's great drama, and help to make the whole production a thing of infinite delight to God. Our own personal story is a unique mini-dramatic production, wheels within wheels, of God's great drama. There has never been anyone, nor will there ever be, whose story is played out in quite the way that ours is.

Each of us takes the lead role, with our own supporting cast under the direction of our loving heavenly Father.

7. Drama in Bible-times and the early church

In the western world theatres, as we would recognise them, did not exist until the Greeks began to use drama to celebrate their gods.

The words we have for drama, theatre, comedy, tragedy, dialogue, character, chorus, episode, mime and scene are all Greek in origin. However, drama has probably always existed in some form throughout history as people have sought to worship their gods in ritual and ceremony, express their stories, both true and fictional, and their life dramas with all their hopes and fears.

Drama has given people opportunities to explain events and portray life's tragedies, or its more humorous and absurd aspects. Rarely separate from each other, drama, song and dance emerge from every culture, anchored in everyday life, religion, folklore and symbolic language, that helps a community understand itself. Scratch the surface of every continent, country, people group and tribe to discover drama in a huge variety of forms, each with its own distinctive origin and flavour.

Praise poems

Preceding and alongside the Greek Empire God's people existed in Canaan and flourished under his hand. Drama formed part of their life too, although it could not have been more different from Greek drama with its elements of pagan worship. In Old Testament times, praise poems celebrated the righteousness of God before other nations and were an exhortation to Israel to remain faithful. Sometimes poems were recited to commemorate a national victory, with their focus firmly on God. These were an exciting, dramatic presentation of the adventure of God's choice, intervention, deliverance and providence. The song of Moses, Miriam and the Israelites is an example.

> Then Moses and the Israelites sang this song to the Lord: I will sing to the Lord, for he is highly exalted. The horse and its rider he has hurled into the sea. The Lord is my strength and my song; he has become my salvation. He is my God, and I will praise him, my father's God, and I will exalt him. The Lord is a warrior; The Lord is his name. Pharaoh's chariots and his army he has hurled into the sea. The best of Pharaoh's officers are drowned in the Red Sea. The deep waters have covered them; they sank to the depths like a stone. (From Exodus 15:1-18)

The song of Deborah recorded in Judges 5 is one of the oldest poems in the Bible, performed to commemorate the dramatic story of the triumph of Jael over the powerful Canaanite general, Sisera. This poem gives insight into the life and times of Deborah and her contemporaries, and tells us that there were groups of roaming minstrels who encouraged travellers, rich and poor, to remember the past heroic achievements of the Lord and his warriors. It is unlikely that these graphic word pictures were just spoken or sung, but more probable that they were accompanied by action and dance.

> You who ride on white donkeys, sitting on your saddle blankets, and you who walk along the road, consider the voice of the singers at the watering places. They recite the righteous acts of the Lord, the righteous acts of his warriors in Israel. (Judges 5:10–11)

Psalms

These are a collection of praise songs and prayers, for both corporate and individual use. They were often sung, accompanied by stringed instruments such as harp, lute and lyre. Some psalms were written for teaching purposes, specific thanksgiving, festivals, worship, request for God's help in time of trouble, confession or an enactment of a historical event. They were written over a period of time, many by unknown writers. King David wrote many of the psalms included in our Bible. Under his administration temple liturgy began to take shape. Psalm writers followed a highly developed poetic tradition and their composition shows a tendency for the dramatic, enjoyed by those who read, recited or listened to them. A brief look at the situations in which psalms were presented shows people whose hearts were set on God, with plenty of opportunity to dramatise their contents as they praised, worshipped, petitioned and thanked God together.

After the temple in Jerusalem was completed by King

Solomon, each year Jews from far and wide attended the three special festivals of the Passover - Feast of Unleavened Bread, the Feast of Weeks and the Feast of Tabernacles (Deuteronomy 16:16). Pilgrims chorally spoke or sung psalms or songs of ascent (Psalms 120–134) as they processed up to the temple, motivating them to praise God and prepare for worship. Psalm 120 begins with people acknowledging that they live far away from God in his temple, and Psalm 134 ends with a call to the Levites from departing worshippers that they should continue to praise God in the sanctuary. Such a God-soaked entrance and exit of thousands of worshippers must have been dramatic and impressive.

Some psalms were recited with response lines for people to join in during the liturgy. Psalm 136 is an example of this and was probably led by a levitical praise or song leader, with a choir or general worshippers joining in the refrain. Other liturgical psalms were sung or spoken antiphonally, with two sections of a choir taking turns phrase by phrase.

However difficult, we need to understand these tiny printed words in our Bibles, and see them come alive in our imaginations, vibrant with noisy shouts of joy and acclamation, repetitive liturgy calling down the greatness of God in a celebration of praise with incense, huge choirs, orchestras and thousands of worshippers, all wrapped in the glory of the presence of God.

That's drama!

Festivals

From the earliest period of Israel's history, Jews observed the Sabbath and festivals as directed by God. These included the Feast of Unleavened Bread, Firstfruits, Weeks, Trumpets, Day of Atonement, Tabernacles, New Moon and later, around the fifth century BC, Purim and Dedication or Lights. Festivals were connected with the seasons of the farmer's year in Canaan and men were expected to attend their local shrine to present their offerings to God. After the seventh century BC, the main festivals were held in Jerusalem at the temple. Festivals were times of thanksgiving to God for harvests, and occasions to remember and celebrate special events in Israel's history. They were opportunities for huge rejoicing and feasting, many of them played out in dramatic symbolism and role play.

Even fasting had significant symbolism, signalling repentance to those watching. While fasting, people did not eat or drink. They tore their clothes and dressed in sackcloth and threw dust or ashes on their heads. They would leave their hair uncombed and their bodies unwashed. These symbols dramatized their grief for sin and their inability to make themselves right with God unless he graciously relented.

Prophets

Old Testament prophets proclaimed God's messages to people and also dramatised those messages in memorable ways.

1. Sometimes, God highlighted ordinary everyday articles to make his message relevant and meaningful, and the prophets used these to tell God's words to his people. Prophetic drama, using both verbal and visual images, was demonstrated by Amos. Amos was from Tekoa in the southern kingdom of Judah. Amos prophesied

during the reign of Uzziah of Judah and Jereboam II of Israel, mainly between 760–750 BC. He was skilled with words, with good understanding of his times and history. God sent Amos to the northern kingdom of Israel to announce God's judgement on his people.

This is what he showed me: The Lord was standing by a wall that had been built true to plumb, with a plumb-line in his hand. And the Lord asked me, 'What do you see, Amos?' 'A plumb-line,' I replied. Then the Lord said, 'Look, I am setting a plumb-line among my people Israel; I will spare them no longer.'

(Amos 7:7–8)

This is what the Sovereign Lord showed me: a basket of ripe fruit. 'What do you see, Amos?' he asked. 'A basket of ripe fruit,' I answered. Then the Lord said to me, 'The time is ripe for my people Israel; I will spare them no longer.' (Amos 8:1–2)

2. God used a specific place to initiate a prophecy and dramatize his message through Jeremiah. Jeremiah began prophesying in Judah halfway through the reign of Josiah (640–609 BC). He continued giving God's words through the reigns of Jehoahaz, Jehoiakim, Jehoiachin and Zedekiah. In anguish, Jeremiah prophesied the destruction of the kingdom of Judah to God's unrepentant people. Jeremiah's struggles to live through these stormy times and bring God's words to his people, with hope for the future, are open and evident in his book.

This is the word that came to Jeremiah from the Lord: 'Go down to the potter's house, and there I will give you my message.' So I went down to the potter's house, and I saw him working at the wheel. But the pot he was shaping from the clay was marred in his hands; so the potter formed it into another pot, shaping it as seemed best to him. Then the word of the Lord came to me: 'O house of Israel, can I not do with you as this potter does?' declares the Lord. 'Like clay in the hands of the potter, so are you in my hand, O house of Israel.' (Jeremiah 18:1–6)

3. God even used a prophet's whole life to dramatize and tell Israel how he felt about them. Hosea's life portrayed a love story of a man who took a faithless wife, who betrayed him. His life drama echoed God's deep heart love for a faithless Israel, betrayed time without number. Hosea's life drama has beauty, ugliness, heartache, tenderness, pathos, good and bad, and God's love and faithfulness to a faithless people shine through every word and dramatic act.

The word of the Lord that came to Hosea, son of Beeri during the reigns of Uzziah, Jotham, Ahaz and Hezekiah, kings of Judah, and during the reign of Jereboam, son of Joash king of Israel: When the Lord began to speak through Hosea, the Lord said to him, 'Go, take to yourself an adulterous wife and children of unfaithfulness, because the land is guilty of the vilest adultery in departing from the Lord.' So he married Gomer, daughter of Diblaim, and she conceived and bore him a son.' (Hosea 1:1-3)

Starting just before New Testament times some theatres were built by the Romans in Palestine but the plays performed were Greek-style, based on Roman classical gods and mythology. As these plays celebrated false gods, devout Jews would not have attended their performances. God's people understood well that drama could be used for ungodly or immoral purposes, but they also knew the thrill and excitement of drama used to convey God's truth and the delights of his care.

Jesus was born into a Jewish family, whose appreciation of the great dramatic traditions of their faith would have been eagerly absorbed by a small boy growing up at that time. Most children love acting and many of their games are composed of situation drama. These have always helped children to safely tackle real-life issues and work out their responses. Jesus' reference to children playing at weddings and funerals in the market place would have struck a memorable chord with his listeners from their own childhood experiences, and probably his own. As he taught, Jesus painted dramatic pictures in people's imaginations. They may not always have understood the meaning of his teaching in stories and parables, but their drama and humour was unforgettable.

Everything that Jesus did both privately with his disciples, and publicly, carried an element of drama and wherever possible crowds of people watched and listened to his performance, amazed at his teaching, power, compassion and authority.

After feeding more than five thousand people, Jesus withdrew from the crowd's claims and expectations of him, and prayed alone in the mountains (John 6:16–24). His disciples set off across the lake for Capernaum, but were overtaken by bad weather. Several miles into their voyage,

Jesus caught up with them, walking on the water. When they realised it was Jesus and pulled him into the boat, they suddenly and immediately found themselves safely at their destination. Those who had been present at the miracle of the picnic on the hill were mystified as to where Jesus was. They had watched his disciples set out across the lake without him. When they found Jesus at Capernaum on the other side of the lake, he was with his friends. No one knew how he had arrived, as only one boat had left the shore the previous evening. Jesus' reason for his dramatic mode of transport is given in John 6:25–40. It focused attention fully on him and he gave his teaching point from the breaking of the bread and fish, that he alone is the bread of life.

The miracles that Jesus performed were often accompanied by high drama for many to see and wonder at (Luke 8:26–39). The healing of the man who lived among the tombs is one example. If yours had been the responsibility for tending those pigs, you would not have forgotten that particular performance. Another is the healing of the blind man recorded in John 9. Did Jesus need to mix mud with spit and rub it on the man's eyes to effect his healing? No, of course not. Jesus used the dramatic effect of this healing to further the discussion about his true identity and mission. The furore that ensued set people wondering and arguing and resulted in the man, formerly blind, being excommunicated from the synagogue for telling the truth. Afterwards, Jesus gently brought the man to faith in him (John 9:35–38).

Jesus took on the dramatic presentation and fulfilment of Old Testament prophecy when he rode into Jerusalem in his final days (Zechariah 9:9; Luke 19:28–44). Jesus could have

just asked to borrow anyone's colt for his purpose, but even
the finding of this animal became part of the drama. Jesus'
enactment, recalling Israel's greatest days (1 Kings 1:32–48),
was a silent performance with public proclamation. No
words were needed for his audience. They knew from
Scripture that this unbroken, unridable animal carried the
chosen Son of David, and King, and they received him rap-
turously.

The trial, death on a cross and resurrection of the sinless
Son of God must be the greatest drama ever, and is very
simply and starkly portrayed for us in Scripture. For those
who have grown up knowing Bible stories, it's easy to lose
sight of their dramatic impact on those who lived through
those times, whether believers or not. Jesus could have chosen to return to his Father in heaven at a time when he was
on his own, but he chose to have an audience witness his
ascension.

Can you imagine their open-mouthed response, even
after all they had already seen, as Jesus rose from the
ground and disappeared into the clouds?

We are not told that early believers used drama in the
way we tend to think of it being used in church. They were
ordinary people like us with ordinary jobs, families and
homes to run, but their belief in Jesus as Lord brought
drama right into their lives and exposed others to it also.

Who needs a play of three acts to explain the coming of
the promised Holy Spirit and as a means of evangelism
when his presence is evident in fire, wind, speech, great
power and changed lives (Acts 2)? Peter and John could not
have had a more public place to perform than the temple
gate. The healing of the crippled beggar was dramatic, and

astounded those watching (Acts 3). Reading the Acts of the Apostles and noting every dramatic incident as God built his church, and every miraculous sign and wonder performed through the power of the Holy Spirit, makes the most interesting play appear dull by comparison. God certainly knows how to use drama through people's lives to the best and fullest effect, and these are still the best kind of dramas today.

The newly emerging church composed of Gentiles and Jews who had been converted, worshipped Jesus as Lord, and God as their Father. They embraced God's continuing plan for his people and delighted in a full and glorious heritage of Scripture, which included prophecies, psalms and songs, as well as discovering new forms of worship and structure. Several centuries after New Testament times there is plenty of documented evidence to show that Christian drama existed in many different forms. It is probable, although not verifiable, that these had been developed as the early church grew.

Today, those who are working through the medium of drama with church-based groups need no convincing that drama has a helpful role in teaching, worship and ritual, and evangelism. Used carefully and prayerfully drama can, and must, reflect the full radiance of biblical truth. The Bible is full of drama, both comedy and tragedy, and the stories of the people written about amazingly tell how things really were. Drama can also be used to tell our own stories in the context of our life in God, including humour. Fun and laughter are part of our whole life, mixed in with the good and the difficult parts, leaking out sometimes when we least expect. They too can be reflected in our faith in God. Drama is not dead. It can never die while people exist because the warp and weft of drama is in our souls.

8. Using drama with under 5s

Under-fives change almost before our eyes.

Their physical, mental and emotional development changes faster than at any other time in their lives. These changes don't take place at the same pace in any individual child, and in a group of under-fives the challenges provided for parents, leaders and helpers is exhaustive, in every sense of the word!

The following points may help you in your thinking and preparation for using drama. Make opportunity to think and talk them through with your helpers and add your own ideas. The key words to this section are, keep it simple!

Choosing your materials

- For toddlers and very young children, drama begins with the simplest forms e.g. games and action rhymes such as *Peep-bo, Round and round the garden, This is the way the lady rides, Incey Wincey Spider,* etc. Rhymes similar to these can be used with many simple Bible stories and characters.

- When choosing a story for drama, make sure it's age-appropriate.
- Knowing your children well will help you develop cus-tom-written rhymes and drama, using their own abili-ties, qualities and characters to maximize enjoyment and learning.
- Use familiar, simple storylines for drama e.g. home, play-group or nursery, family, friends, animals, doctor, funny things that happen to us.
- Use themes and well-known characters, human or animal, to express feelings of happiness, comfort, anger, being sorry, love, etc.
- Dramatized Bible stories have the same strengths as other stories for learning opportunities and enjoyment.
- Limit the story for your drama to a simple sequence, or single event.
- Time sequences mean little to young children, e.g. yesterday, tomorrow, next week/year, last week/year etc., and are irrelevant.
- State things as they are or keep explanations very short.
- Use very little prose and plenty of action words.
- Look for opportunities to include anticipation, tension and delivery to your drama.

EXAMPLE: JESUS CALMS THE STORM

Mark 4:35–41.
The little boat sailed up and down, gently on the sea.
Jesus lay in the boat, sleeping peacefully.

Suddenly, the thunder crashed,
Then the lightning dashed and flashed.
The noisy wind blew loud and long.
Though Jesus' friends were very strong,
They couldn't row the little boat.
They said, 'This boat will hardly float!'
The little boat was nearly lost in a great big wave.
Jesus' friends woke him up, 'Jesus! Won't you save?'
Jesus told the wind and waves, 'It's time to stop.
    Right now!'
And they did! But Jesus' friends didn't know quite how.
Once again, the little boat sailed gently on the sea.
Jesus said, 'Why be afraid? You're in the boat with me!'

- Write out your story-drama line by line. This will help you keep it brief and action-packed.
- Check out up-to-date Bible story books and children's Bibles for ideas and styles.
- Don't use unfamiliar vocabulary or long words.

EXAMPLE: PETER AND THE ANGEL

Acts 12:1–17.
You will need: Newspapers; sticky tape; scissors; table.
In advance: Cut newspaper sheets into long fringes. Stick the fringes so that they hang down from the table.

Children can take turns to be Peter and the angel. Remaining children can be Peter's friends.

Peter was asleep in prison.
Peter under the table behind the newspaper fringe.
Jesus sent an angel to help Peter.

Angel wakes Peter.
Peter followed the angel.
Peter gets up and follows the angel.
Peter went to his friends' house.
Peter knocks at the door.
They were pleased to see him.
Group hug.
Jesus had more work for Peter to do. Jesus sent an angel to help Peter escape from prison.

- Use direct, clear words, without euphemisms e.g. not 'the lady lost her husband'; but 'the lady's husband had died' (Bible story of the widow's offering Mark 12:41–44).
- Try to identify children's different learning styles and make space for these so that everyone can be involved.
- Remember children's attention span is roughly one minute for every one year of their age.
- It may be possible to introduce some of children's own spontaneous ideas for drama.

Props and other simple teaching aids

- Most young children enjoy dressing up, but don't force those who don't want to. Try to work out reasons for refusal e.g. fear of taking off clothes, losing identity or something important to them, etc. Know your children well and be prepared with something else these children can do or hold so that they don't feel excluded.
- Think what simple props, explanations and actions could be added to create and set the scene for drama.
- Think what sounds children could create to add dramatic

impact to your chosen drama e.g. rain, wind, waves, crying, laughing, etc.
- Use repetitive words, phrases or actions for children to join in as the drama progresses.
- Work out in advance props for helpers to use to stimulate interest and promote the drama.

EXAMPLE: ZACCHAEUS FINDS A FRIEND

Luke 19:1–10.
You will need: Two helpers (one tall and one shorter); twigs, leaves and green material; story-drama of Zacchaeus. Bind twigs and leaves around wrists and head of the tall helper, the 'tree'. Drape the green material around them. While the short story-drama is being narrated Zacchaeus, the shorter helper, can act out receiving the money, trying to see over the crowds, jumping into the 'tree', surprise and joy at Jesus' request, and repaying the money to astonished people.

- Think of objects for children to hold and show in a Bible drama or an activity to support a Bible story.

EXAMPLE: GOD ANSWERS HANNAH'S PRAYER

Samuel 1:1–2:21.
You will need: Paper tissues; mirror; calendar; baby shawl; paper heart; different-sized children's clothes. Give items to different children to hold and pass around the group.
Hannah was very upset because she had no baby. (Paper tissues.)

Eli the priest said God had heard her prayers and would give her what she asked. (Mirror. Everyone can smile at their reflection.)

Hannah had to wait. (Calendar. Name months of the year aloud.)

At last, Samuel was born. (Baby shawl.)

When Samuel was a little boy, Hannah took him to help Eli the priest. (Paper heart. Everyone can wave goodbye as they let it go.)

Hannah took new clothes for Samuel as he grew bigger. (Assorted children's clothes.)

God answered Hannah's prayer. Hannah said thank you to God. (Everyone clap.)

* Give actions to your stories, demonstrating them for children to copy.
* Sung drama can add interest. Put simple words to familiar nursery or action rhyme tunes. Demonstrate simple actions to accompany the song-drama.

EXAMPLE: JESUS GOES BACK TO HEAVEN

Luke 24:50–53; Acts 1:7–11; Matthew 28:20.

Make a standing circle with children. Sing the rhyme to the tune *Frère Jacques*.

Our friend Jesus, (You sing. Children repeat the line with you.) Hold hands and swing arms.

Where's he gone? (You sing. Children repeat the line with you.) Shade eyes, looking up.

He's gone back to heaven. (You sing. Children repeat the line with you.) Hold hands and swing arms.

He loves us. (You sing. Children repeat the line with you.) Make a group hug.

- Simple puppets for children to hold or use for specific characters can be helpful e.g. craft sticks with faces drawn on them, finger stickers, wooden spoons, paper plates on craft sticks, etc.
- Use a hand puppet yourself to dramatize a story. Some young children are more comfortable when the action, and feelings are expressed through a puppet character.
- Think about using mime to express different emotions of the characters in the drama. Children can copy these.
- Face painting can be fun if children are willing, or use helpers' faces for painting. Provide plenty of mirrors.
- Paper plate masks are easily made and some children may feel safer in character while using them.
- Keep props simple and safe.

Explaining to the children

- When using mime teach the simple expressions you have chosen for your characters beforehand. Children will be able to copy you and join in as the drama and story progress. Use mirrors for children to see their own expressions.
- Practise at home your simple instructions to children in a mirror, and smile, with eye contact. When we concentrate, we tend to frown.
- Prepare children before beginning drama, repeating instructions, but don't take so long over it that they lose interest.

- Teach any repetitive words, phrases or actions before beginning, and create a signal so children know when they're coming.

Doing it

- Don't rush! Speak slowly and clearly.
- Use plenty of expression when speaking and encourage children to do the same. Have them repeat words or phrases back to you, copying the same expression and actions.
- Some children may have difficulty putting words and actions together. Encourage, but don't single children out for attention.
- Some children are developing vivid imaginations and may need reassurance.
- Very young children have not yet developed the ability to work together and work better alongside each other. With help and encouragement, some may be able to take a particular role or character, but will probably still find it hard to interact with others.
- Don't have favourite children. Learn to love and include them all.
- Encourage independent thinking, or bring attention back with a question e.g. What do you think would happen if…?
- Watch for children who lose concentration, give up or wander off. Try to re-include them by giving them something specific to do, or assign a helper to be with them.
- Don't push reluctant children to take active parts, but encourage them to hold something important or integral

to the drama.
- Give plenty of genuine praise and show by example how to compliment and appreciate others.
- Don't over-dramatize or frighten children.
- Watch out for children who may be frightened by the strength of their emotions.

And finally, don't forget to have fun, and include humour where possible. Don't allow children to laugh at each other, but make plenty of opportunity to laugh together.

9. Using drama with 5-9s

Such is the intensity of concentration on key stages in education that in some schools there is little time or scope for activities such as drama. Many of the benefits listed in our introduction would be immensely helpful in classroom settings to teachers and pupils alike. Drama is a shared experience and can be used to explore subjects and issues right across the curriculum, providing children with many skills, understanding and knowledge.

Happily, most church-based activities are not limited by such strict curricula and drama can find a place in kids' clubs, after school clubs, Sunday schools and other settings where children meet to learn, socialize and have fun together. Church is not a place, but the people or family of God, and within this family children can learn about God and each other, give and receive love and affirmation, enjoy life together and learn to share it with those as yet outside. Drama is an ideal tool to help achieve these aims in relaxed and fun ways.

The differences between a five-year-old and a nine-year-old are immense, and leaders might initially feel that this range is too great to enable drama to flourish well. It's right to consider the differences, not just between the youngest and oldest children, but in the development of children of the same age throughout the range. Every child is unique and leaders need to know individual children well. However, a group that has a spread of ability, experience and age can be helpful and is not always the disadvantage one might initially think. Children learn from each other as well as from adults. In an accepting, caring environment such as the church family, where they are given an example of how to listen to and respect each other, drama can be a hugely satisfying experience for everyone.

Children in this age group are well placed to begin exploring drama:

- They are able to understand and appreciate that drama is more than just doing actions.
- They are beginning to be aware of their own feelings, emotions, thoughts and attitudes.
- They know that these are sometimes expressed in good and helpful ways, and sometimes not.
- Many of them will have already begun their own journey with God, or be willing to consider it.
- The growing importance of the peer group provides a natural pool of opportunity for children to appreciate each other, become more tolerant of each other and to develop positive attitudes.
- Although increasingly affected by their peers, they are mostly not yet too inhibited to enjoy and learn through

well-thought-out drama.

- Children can work together as a team and not just along-side each other.
- With encouragement, children generally have sufficient language skills to be able to put their thoughts into words.
- Growing independence enables them to offer their own creative ideas to a welcoming and non-judgemental forum.
- Motor skills are increasingly well developed and can be channelled positively through drama.
- Even children at the younger end of the group are becoming less egocentric and more interested in the world around them, its peoples and problems.
- Children are getting used to responding appropriately to instructions.
- Children love to have fun!
- Add some ideas of your own:
-
-

At its best, through drama, actors draw both their fellow actors and the audience into their story. They make it believable, yet anchored in the real world through its characters or actions. Drama is a shared experience, giving of one's self through a character and calling for a response of minds and hearts, freely given. This can make some children aware of their vulnerability, and needs to be handled sensitively. Don't allow children to laugh at each other, but look for opportunities to affirm and offer support.

There will always be some children who, even with the greatest encouragement, will not be comfortable with acting, being the centre of attention or showing their emotions publicly. This may be a reflection of family background. Sadly, some children have been made to feel inadequate, had too much expected of them or been over-criticised, making them unwilling to try anything new. Reluctance may also be part of their character, personality and learning styles. All these are yet more reasons for getting to know children well. With careful planning and plenty of encouragement, ways can be found to increase children's confidence, enabling them to become involved and given their own vital and important role, acting or non-acting.

Where do I start?

- Get to know the children in your group, not just in the normal meeting situation, but in their home and yours, and in other settings.
- Think about the space you meet in e.g. size, shape, light and air, flooring, proximity to others, acoustics, storage space for props. Most meeting spaces can accommodate some forms of drama but it may be possible to swap rooms with another group occasionally, meet elsewhere or even outdoors.
- Drama has many varied forms and can be used on a regular basis without becoming boring or routine. If you decide that children will benefit from its use, arrange to meet with your team and talk through some of the issues from this book. Listen to their ideas, points of view, doubts and fears. Face the challenges and remain positive. If possible, begin to plan some simple drama.
- If you use the *Children's Ministry Teaching Programme* you will know that some form of simple drama is included in

most sessions. With your team, look ahead for these and work them out with your own children in mind.

- Ask individual team members to each list stories, songs, rhymes or topics they consider suitable for drama. Team members can choose one each to try and write a simple drama from it using their own ideas, or some of those listed below. Invite everyone to keep their effort short, interesting and action-packed. You may not achieve immediate success, and will need to be sensitive to people's feelings, but you will gain ideas and confidence. Improvements come with practice, and unexpected and surprising gifts can develop. Also be prepared to look outside your immediate team for input and ideas.

- Write out your chosen drama, making sure it's neither too complex nor too long, has an attention grabbing beginning, action and a satisfactory end. Check that your team is happy and enthusiastic about it. Work out any actions you want children to copy. Learn them well so that you can teach them to children. Discuss ways to add interest or extra dimensions of drama through music, sound or special effects, face painting, dressing up, props, fabric, pictures or scenery, etc.

- Create a role for everyone, whether acting or helping create the drama in other ways.

- Start from where you and the children in your group are, and take it slowly. Beginners will not feel confident with having lines to learn or standing out alone. For younger or less confident children, try together an action rhyme or expressive mime to a line-by-line narrated drama supporting a Bible story (see under 5s example).

EXAMPLE: QUEEN ESTHER FINDS A WAY

Esther 4–8.

Write out the words. Fix them where everyone can see. Demonstrate the actions with words and repeat together.

God helped Esther find a way Everyone kneel.

To save his people on that day. Clasp hands together.

King Xerxes might be very great, Bow down to the ground.

And Haman, full of powerful hate, Shake fist and scowl.

But God is greater than them all, Lift hands to God.

And answers when his people call. Stand with lifted hands.

Great men or kings, they cannot stand After the words, blow through the mouth.

When God decides to move his hand. Raise clenched fists.

- A warm-up game or activity can relax children, help them gain awareness of facial expressions, body movement, interaction, and speech. These can be fun on their own, but can also lead easily into drama.

EXAMPLE: SHOE SHUFFLE

You will need: A child's soft shoe or slipper.

Make a seated circle. Children are to pass the shoe around the circle without using their hands. If the shoe lands on the floor it must be retrieved by the child who dropped it, and passed back two places before starting again. These rules apply for each round as different body parts are used to pass the shoe.

First round: Use elbows.

Second round: Use feet.

Third round: Use knees.

Fourth round: Use feet.

Fifth round: Use chins and shoulders.

Choose a different child each time to begin the round. They can choose the shoe's direction round the circle. Encourage everyone to co-operate with each other, passing the shoe carefully and slowly. Praise and affirm those who are helpful to others. Have group applause, without using hands, at the end of each round.

EXAMPLE: MIRROR MOODS

Alone, in pairs or groups, using mirrors, encourage everyone to think of a time when they might experience one of these different moods or emotions, and find facial and body expressions for it: Boredom, fear, anger, panic, excitement, sadness, hope, loneliness, nervousness, joy, envy, love. These can be demonstrated in turn to the group. Applaud each attempt.

EXAMPLE: JOKING APART

Use a joke book to demonstrate how to tell a joke and deliver the punch line satisfactorily. Have everyone choose a joke and tell it to the group. Be encouraging!

EXAMPLE: FUNNY BONES

Humour is very important. Check out your local library for a copy of the *Complete Junior Choice* CD. Play the Laughing Policeman song for everyone to join in.

- Group characters also work well with beginners. From your chosen drama, assign one character, spoken lines, rhyme or actions to each group with a helper to lead them. Orchestrate the drama in sequence.

- Don't regularly choose the same more confident children to take lead parts even though they may always be the first to volunteer. When planning, make every effort to be inclusive and genuinely generous with praise.

- As children become more used to drama, listen to their own ideas and acknowledge each one carefully so contributors feel valued and important. As confidence and enthusiasm grow, original ideas and thoughtful outlook sometimes come from those we might consider less gifted or vocal.

- When exploring drama and story-lines, allow time for children to think about the characters involved. Talk through with them the thoughts and feelings that might be expressed. Ask questions e.g. What do you think he was like? Shy? Confident? Happy? Unhappy? Why do you think she did that? What do you think she would have done next? Don't be too quick to impose your own ideas.

- Demonstrate how imagination, improvisation and freedom of expression can create a living drama from ordinary or dramatic situations. Let children practise some for themselves in pairs or small groups.

EXAMPLE: GOD HELPED THE ISRAELITES

Exodus 13:17–15;21.
Imagine you are part of an Israelite family and the sea has

just opened up in front of you. What should you do? Is it safe to go through? What else could you do? How do you feel? What if some of you want to go forward, but one person is afraid to move? How could you persuade them? Talk through the scene with children, naming those in their families, and what they might do in a similar situation. Make small family groups for children to work out their ideas and act out the scene.

- Lead firmly, speaking slowly without shouting. Repeat instructions, and smile!
- If first attempts don't go well, don't give up. With your team, identify the reasons and work on them.

Where can I get ideas for drama?

- Bible stories and psalms.
- Look for simple drama opportunities with Bible memory verses.
- Fiction stories and biographies.
- TV and radio programmes.
- Children's poems e.g. *The Day I Fell Down the Toilet and other poems* by Steve Turner published by Lion, *Please Mrs Butler* by Allan Ahlberg published by Puffin, *Wish you were here* by Colin McNaughton published by Walker Books.
- True-life situations familiar to children from family life, friendships and other relationships, school, etc. featuring emotions, conflict/resolution, moods.
  Examples: What happened when …
… I borrowed Dad's foreign coin collection and took it to

    school.

... my best friend fell in the fish pond.

... I got locked in the bathroom/stuck in a lift.

... there was a fire in the staffroom at school.

... I kicked my football over next-door's fence.

... Mum finished the shopping in the supermarket and found she'd left her purse at home.

... I was sitting in the bath and a big, hairy spider climbed through the overflow.

... I found a wallet someone had dropped.

... Auntie Jane found a mouse in the airing cupboard.

- Music CDs, BBC sound effects CDs, songs. Explore your local library CD resource for ideas. These can be used to support an existing story-drama or to begin ideas for a new one. Let children listen to your chosen music. What does this music make you think of? Encourage everyone to contribute, asking individual questions if necessary.

- Look for suitable pictures in newspapers and magazines to get children thinking, 'What happened next?' Video clips can be used in the same way. Freeze-frame the clip at an exciting point and invite ideas to be acted out.

How can I turn these ideas into drama?

- Use improvisation and role play to help children think what it was like to be in a particular situation. They can act out their ideas. Why do you think the Ethiopian Philip met was reading the Scriptures? Why was he, a foreigner, in Jerusalem? What do you think happened after he met Philip? (Acts 8:26:40). How did Zacchaeus feel when Jesus called him down from the tree? How do you think he began to make friends? (Luke 19:1–10.)

These ideas can form the actual Bible story, or create a supporting dramatic activity.

Example: Jesus heals a lame man

John 5.
You will need: Blue material or sheet; bubble wrap.
Lay the blue material over a length of bubble wrap. Sit everyone on either side.
The pool at Bethesda sometimes bubbled, like a jacuzzi. Sick or disabled people believed that if they could get into the bubbling water, they would be made well. They waited, watching carefully. What would happen if you ... Could run and jump?
Were blind and had a helper? No helper?
Were lame or paralysed and had a helper? No helper?
Have two adults hold the ends of the material covering the bubble wrap.
Let's pretend this is the pool at Bethesda. Are you waiting, and watching the water? After a few moments, helpers begin to ripple the material upwards, revealing the bubble wrap. **Jump in quickly, if you can!** Children jump onto the bubble wrap. Repeat several times.

• Memory verse opportunities for drama.

Example: Daniel in danger

Daniel 6.
Memory Verse: Do what is right and good in the Lord's sight. Deuteronomy 6:18.

Make two groups. The first group can roar like lions while the second group face them and shout the memory verse aloud. Then swap over.

EXAMPLE: DAVID ASKS GOD FOR HELP

1 Samuel 30:1–20; Nahum 1:7.
You will need: Newspapers; paper; marker pen; bin liner.
In advance: Scrunch up newspaper to make a pile of paper balls. Write out the memory verse and reference.

Have everyone read the memory verse together. David was in trouble with King Saul, in trouble with his enemies, and in trouble with his own men. He trusted God to help and God answered his prayers. Have children read the verse in turn, while others throw paper balls at them.

- Fiction stories and biographies. Check out *Ten Boys Who Changed the World* and *Ten Girls Who Changed the World* by Irene Howat, published by Lightkeepers. Choose an exciting or interesting day in the life of one character. With your team, write a short, action-packed script and think through possible actions. Read both the story and your script dramatically to children and listen to their ideas for presentation. What extra dimensions would sound effects, costumes and scenery bring?
- Write simple scripts for child readers or adults to narrate expressively. Children can mime actions.

EXAMPLE: KING SOLOMON ASKS GOD FOR WISDOM

1 Kings 3; 4:29–34; 10:1–9.
You will need: Card crown; cloak, doll; sword; cardboard boxes.

Choose King David, Solomon, two mothers and a guard.

When King David died, his son Solomon became King. Transfer crown and cloak from David to Solomon.

Solomon was young, and felt weighed down by the job of being King. Pile Solomon with boxes.

In a dream, God asked Solomon what he would like to be given. Solomon sleeps and snores.

Solomon asked God to make him wise so he would know the right things to do, and be able to do them. Remove boxes from Solomon.

God was pleased with Solomon. Everyone can clap and cheer.

Two mothers with one baby came to see Solomon. One mother holds the doll.

They argued over who was the baby's mother. Mothers hold and snatch the doll alternately.

Solomon didn't know who was the baby's real mother. Solomon holds up his hands, and sighs.

Solomon told a guard to cut the baby in half. Guard holds the sword over the doll.

One mother asked Solomon not to do it. One mother kneels to Solomon and pleads.

The second mother told Solomon it was only fair. Second mother folds her arms, and nods.

Solomon knew the first mother was the baby's real mother. Give doll to first mother.

Solomon knew the real mother would rather give the baby away than see him die. God made Solomon wise. Give God a clap offering.

All applaud.

- Write action rhymes on your chosen theme to be spoken aloud together, as one voice, pairs, in turn or building from a single voice to everyone speaking together.

EXAMPLE: SAMUEL ANOINTS DAVID AS KING

1 Samuel 16:1–13.
In advance: Write out the words of the rhyme.
  Read the rhyme together. In pairs, children can make up actions to the words. Have each pair show their actions while others repeat the rhyme aloud.

Outside in, or inside out,
I can whisper, I can shout,
God's the One who sees and knows
All of me, from brains to toes.
Young or old, tall or thin,
Wide as a house, small as a pin.
God doesn't look at what you see,
But at the treasure inside of me.

- Find songs on children's CDs e.g. *12 New Children's Praise Songs, volumes 1-4* (Children's Ministry). Children can help create actions for them as they sing.
- Review stories in music e.g. *Peter and the Wolf, Carnival of the Animals* and help them decide their actions to accompany the music.
- Have helpers act out your chosen drama and pre-teach a rhyming couplet, phrase or actions to children to speak together at a given signal during the drama. This idea can also be used as a Bible story follow-up rhyme.

EXAMPLE: JESUS TEACHES ABOUT PRAYER

Matthew 6:13; 14:23; 18:20; Mark 1:35.

You will need: Clocks.

When can we talk to God? *(Any time.)* Beginning at midnight, show how to turn the hands, saying the hours until midnight is reached again. Read the rhyme aloud and children can shout out 'Father God' at the end of each verse, jumping up and down three times and clapping.

Who loves us the very best, if we're from the east or from the west? Father God!

Who wants us to know him more, whether we're rich, or whether we're poor? Father God!

When we want to do what's right, who will help us win the fight? Father God!

When we're faced with something new, who will show us what to do? Father God!

When we're worried in the night, who can comfort with his light? Father God!

Who do we thank for all his care? Who wants to hear our every prayer? Father God!

Who deserves worship and praise? Who can we love through all our days? Father God!

- Give small groups or pairs cards with words, phrases or brief storylines and a limited time to invent their own actions and dramas, with narration and mime if they prefer, role playing a true-life situation.
- Allow children to enjoy experimenting with sounds from ordinary objects, instruments or their voices, to accompany their drama or narration with drama. The human

voice has a huge range of sounds – hissing, blowing, ssh-ing, clicking, sibilant and explosive sounds, tongue rolling, cheek popping etc. to create high/low, loud/soft, shrill/gentle for sad/happy, life/death, embarrass-ment/contentment, etc. Sounds can even replace words altogether to make a soundscape with mime.

EXAMPLE: JESUS HEALS JAIRUS' DAUGHTER.

Luke 8:41–42; 49–56.

Working in small groups, using voices and human sounds, experiment to find sad and happy sounds.

Sadness: **Jairus fell at Jesus' feet. 'Please come to my house. My only daughter who is twelve years old, is dying.' Before they could get there, someone came to say she had died. Jesus still went home with Jairus.** Ideas: Low humming in different pitches. Wailing; Crying at inter-vals. Monotone la-la-la-la. Drone – same note repeated as a background.

Happiness: **Jesus held her hand, and said, 'My child, get up!' And she did!** Ideas: High-pitched, faster sounds and rhythms. Laughter at intervals. Three or four note sequence. Bell ringing sounds. Clapping, cheering. Bring the small groups together. Put their ideas together as a chorale, con-ducting them, letting the intensity ebb and flow.

- Consider using simple puppets to create a drama, or a single puppet operated by an adult.
- Create masks for different characters. Some children will feel more comfortable behind a mask.

- Make your chosen drama into a walk, with stopping places for action.
- Drama combines well with dance, rap and rhythm. These don't have to be complicated and can be incorporated into the theme of your drama for everyone to enjoy.

EXAMPLE: THREE YOUNG MEN DISOBEY THE KING

Daniel 3.

Write out the words of the rap and practise it together to help establish the words and rhythm. In small groups they can work out their own rap and perform them in turn.

They lived in Babylon long ago,
Shadrach, Meshach and Abednego.
Because they served our God alone,
Into the furnace they were thrown.
Old 'nezzar saw our true God's power,
And had them out within the hour.
You people, listen close to me!
Before no idol bow the knee.
Our one true God, he reigns on high.
And that's the truth. It ain't no lie!

- Whether you use your drama just for enjoyment, as a teaching tool, as a presentation to an invited audience, you can add extra dimensions of movement, dance, sound effects, costume, artwork and scenery, props that will include everyone to create a satisfying and memorable experience for all.

10. Using drama with over 9s

It can be baffling when over-nines seem to change – some, almost overnight. Actually, they have always been in the process of change, just like the rest of us. Parents and leaders are sometimes lulled by the five to nine-year-olds less turbulent journey of discovery, enjoyment, energy, sociability and interest. Over-nines are the same children, beginning their turbo-charged pre-pubescent surge, full pelt and unstoppable towards adolescence and adulthood, much like the pre-programmed blast of a booster rocket. If your group of over-nines have not previously enjoyed the benefits of using drama, to begin now may seem like a foolhardy or daunting prospect. A challenge, yes, but not an impossible one.

Let's look briefly at some of the general characteristics of over-nines, as these will affect the introduction, management and success of drama. List the children in your group and take time to consider each one as you read the points noted.

- Over-nines are more aware of themselves than ever before and this can lead to self-consciousness.
- The peer group is very important to them, and the need to conform or fit in is usually very strong.
- The peer group is sometimes used as a base for a challenge against authority, or to exhibit indifference to it.
- Children of this age are beginning to be self-critical and are sensitive to criticism from others, their own peer group or adults.
- They are beginning to be critical of others, especially adults, although they sometimes exhibit double standards.
- They are often idealistic.
- They are beginning to grasp some abstract ideas.
- More and more they expect high standards from adults, with a tendency to see things as black and white.
- They no longer just accept what they are taught as true and will increasingly need to find and own reasons for believing what you say.
- They are able to sort out fact from fiction.
- Girls are faster developers than boys in this age group, both mentally and physically. This shows itself not least in their grasp of ideas. Growth spurts are normal, but can be seen as embarrassing. Hormones and emotions begin to find new boiling points.
- Energy can fluctuate, dipping or soaring suddenly.
- Pop, fashion and football heroes are important to them.
- Add other characteristics you have thought of:
-
-
-

When using drama with any group of people, from the youngest child to the oldest person, it's important to provide security and sensitivity, and to foster it in others. Drama can give a safe, and sometimes pretend, context in which to explore and act out feelings and emotions, situations, attitudes and ideas, and to reflect truth and religious beliefs. When we do this effectively, alone or as a group, the self that we may prefer to hide is often revealed. Some adults and children find this hard, and all revelations of self must be respected by everyone, and seen to be respected.

Consider each child in your group, thinking carefully about their skills and abilities, strengths and weaknesses, learning styles and personal preferences. Even when we know our children well, it's important not to leave them in the niche we have assigned for them, but to encourage and spur them on to try new things, support their efforts and each other.

Where do I start?

- Get to know the children in your group, not just in the normal meeting situation, but in their home and yours, and in other settings. Make these as socially acceptable as possible, working hard to lose any cringe factors. You are the adult and they are a different generation from you. They don't want you to be a child or their best friend, but to find appropriate ways to lead, care, guide, and still have plenty of fun.
- Think about the space you meet in e.g. size, shape, light and air, flooring, proximity to others, acoustics, storage space for props. Most meeting spaces can accommodate

some forms of drama but there are greater opportunities for older children to meet in other places with appropriate supervision. When recruiting regular or extra help, follow your church policy guidelines.

- Arrange to meet with your team to talk through issues raised in this book. Discuss any perceived benefits accruing from the use of drama. Drama has many varied forms and can be used on a regular basis without becoming boring or routine. It can be used to explore the Bible directly; for Bible-story application and life issues; for warm-up and starter activities; for fun; or for performance

- Listen to your team's ideas, points of view, doubts and fears. Face the challenges and remain positive.

- Decide together the purpose of your proposed drama and begin to plan it.

- Children can be gently introduced to drama through a mime game.

EXAMPLE: MIME TIME

Choose several dramatic Bible stories well-known by children e.g. David and Goliath (1 Samuel 17), Jonah and the fish (Jonah 1–4), man lowered through the roof and healed by Jesus (Mark 2:1–12), Zacchaeus and Jesus (Luke 19:1–10).

For each story compose a word list for mime and action e.g. David and Goliath: shepherd, war zone, giant, armour, stone, sling, sword, victory. Make small groups, each with their own word list. Within a given time limit, each group works out actions for the different words. In turn, each group can perform their actions for other groups to guess the words. These don't need to be acted in order. Each group must guess the others' Bible stories.

- Mime is a good introduction to drama as no one has to learn any lines. Children act to narration, which needs to be simple and well written and action packed. Look for opportunities to add sound effects and music. These not only enhance mime but enable non-actors to find satisfying roles.
- Once you have shaped your basic idea, write it out point by point and allow children to work on it with their own ideas. Creativity grows as it is shared, and children will own the final production better if they have had input. Encourage constructive evaluation of their own and others' contributions.
- Find people, from your team or outside, who have experienced drama. Look at any material they may have. You may find a useful nugget to help cultivate ideas. Don't look for the most sensational, impressive or funny presentation. Some of the simplest ideas are the best.
- If children are not used to acting it may be necessary to help them relax enough to express themselves freely. Physical games and action games can help in this warming up process.

EXAMPLE: MAD RELAY

Follow the same pattern as an ordinary shuttle relay. Each team member has to run from behind the starting line to a finish line and back again, passing on a baton to the next team member. In a Mad Relay all team members are numbered and instead of just running, other forms of movement are employed e.g. number ones hop, numbers two and three tie their left and right legs together, number fours balance a book on the head, number five must carry number six. Any variation can be used to release children's inhibitions e.g. clapping, crawling, running on all fours, or assigning different characters/animals/noises for children to act out as they run.

- Children may also need to improve their concentration skills for learning lines, actions and team working. Mental games can help concentration.

EXAMPLE: JUST A MINUTE

A competitor sits in the hot seat and talks for just one minute (or thirty seconds for younger children) on a given topic. Each child or adult helper must talk for the time given without hesitation, deviation or repetition. Provide buzzers or bells to add to the fun. Talk about vocabulary, gabbling too fast, presentation, making yourself heard and understood, etc. Topics for *Just a Minute* are endless: Parties, films I have seen, my favourite foods, worst/best holidays, my first day at school, friends, pets, dentist appointments, etc.

- You will know which children in your group are leaders, and which are followers. Child-leaders, just like their adult counterparts, don't always set a good example for others to follow. They need to be nurtured carefully so that their leadership skills are honed positively, and for good. You will want to encourage dominant characters or those who take a lead in the group, but don't always give them lead parts. Good leaders need to learn how to support and help others. Offer others opportunities to try out lead roles, and encourage all you can.

- Keep up-to-date with children's interests, computer games, sports, music, language, fashions. Find out what films and TV they like to watch. Watch films and programmes yourself that they talk about. All of these will help to produce ideas for drama at some time and will keep you informed and up to date.

- Find out about local drama groups, Christian and non-Christian. Would they be prepared to help you put on a drama workshop? Talk through your goals and ideas with your team and the drama group beforehand, establishing clear objectives and guidelines.

- Look out for suitable shows locally. Discuss the storyline with children and how it might be portrayed. Give everyone (or a small group) a character from the production to think about and discuss. Take the group to see a performance. Check if you can visit backstage. With a prepared list of questions if necessary, talk to the actors, stagehands, producer, etc. Discuss the production with children afterwards. What did they enjoy most / least? What was their character like? Were they believable? How did they make you feel?

- Put on a murder/mystery play/party to give children opportunity to dress up and take on a character. You can either use a ready-made pack or use the format and write your own. You may be able to involve children in script writing. Challenge a group of older children to write a murder mystery play based on Moses and the missing Hebrew (Exodus 2:11–15), revealing how his crime was discovered.

- Knowing your children well will help you find the best ways to encourage their talents, latent or obvious. Don't just focus on acting ability but widen children's appreciation of drama by discussing and demonstrating other connected aspects e.g. costumes, music, props, make-up, sound effects, PA, etc. The aim is for children to have fun and enjoy themselves in a medium they may not have tried before.

- Invite children to talk about their favourite pop or film stars. Provide posters, pictures, videos, clips from Pop Idol etc. Stimulate discussions to help children think about this aspect of drama. Is it fantasy, reality or some of both? Can the stars sing or act live? What helps their character to be perfectly attractive/musical/believable/ cool? (Music, song or script writing, studio production, make-up, hairdressers, clothes, direction, lighting, camerawork, etc.)

- Some leaders fear that introducing drama will invite mayhem. This need not happen. It is important for children to know that you are still in control, even as you listen and encourage new ideas. New skills and disciplines are best learned and practised in an environment of relaxed watchfulness, with plenty of preparation and prayer. Encourage and praise willingness, and expect co-operation. Watch for children who drift to the edge and be ready with positive ways to include them. Speak privately to any child who causes disruption to find the cause of their behaviour.

Where can I get ideas for drama?

- Bible stories and psalms.
- Fiction stories and biographies.
- Missionary characters and exciting/sad/dangerous incidents from their lives.
- TV programmes and films.
- News items and newspapers.
- Music CDs, film themes, BBC sound effects CDs, songs. Explore your own collection and local library.
- Suitable comedy, circus acts, conjuring tricks.
- Poetry. Check out your local library for ideas e.g. *I'm in a Mood Today* and *Football Fever* by John Foster published by Oxford University Press, *Unzip Your Lips* by Paul Cookson published by Macmillan, *Them and Us* by Jennifer Curry published by Red Fox.
- Improvisation and completion of drama-story from true-life situations familiar to children e.g. family life, friendships and other relationships, shopping, computers, hospital, holidays, school, etc. featuring emotions, conflict/resolution, moods. Examples:

1. I was walking to school in the pouring rain. A car went through a huge puddle very fast and drenched me.
2. There was a knock at the door. I opened it and saw my head teacher standing there.
3. I felt the panic start as the lift shuddered to a halt between the third and fourth floors.
4. The noise that woke me in the night was coming from the computer.
5. The curtain moved in an upstairs room of an empty house, and I briefly saw a face at the window.

6. I looked after my neighbour's budgie while she was away, but it died the very first day.
7. I borrowed my brother's camera, but left it on the bus.

How can I turn these ideas into drama?

- The benefits of drama for this age group are as much in the discussion, opportunities for teaching concepts, exploring of situations, building of confidence and generation of ideas as in the drama itself.
- Exploring storylines and the feelings of characters will give greater depth to the drama and help prevent it being a shallow and quickly forgotten experience for everyone.
- Affirm the right of everyone to their opinion as to how a drama should work out. Sometimes a right or wrong way is obvious. Children can learn that at other times it's not so easy to know. Ideas and possibilities need to be worked through to arrive at a decision.
- The best stories portrayed through drama are believable and draw everyone involved in their production, and the audience, into their reality.
- Make opportunities for feedback after the drama is completed to allow children to process their thoughts and feelings, and to grow in them.
- You know your group of children best, and these suggestions may help to generate ideas for drama.
- Newspaper headlines.

EXAMPLE: EXTRA! EXTRA!

Make small groups. Children can cut out a selection of

newspaper headlines, taking three or four for each group.
placing them into groups of three or four e.g. More train
delays! The return of the wild boar. Banana glut forecast!
MPs vote for ban on EU sausages! Children can discuss
their headlines, making a short story from them to be
turned into a two or three minute drama. Helpers can ask
questions to promote discussion, make suggestions if necessary, encourage humour and improvisation, and make
sure everyone is involved in producing ideas. In turn,
groups can act out their dramas.

- Don't be afraid to try classical music along with other
  types of music e.g. excerpts from *Beethoven's Ode to Joy*
  from the *Ninth Symphony* (joy), J Williams *Jurassic Park,
  The Raptor Attack* (fear), Holst's *Neptune* from *The Planet
  Suite* (mystery), H Zimmer's *The Lion King, Under the
  Stars* (loneliness). Help children identify what feelings
  are aroused and offer ideas for action and drama. A simple
  script can be written using an up-to-date, real-life situation or as the background to a Bible drama.
- Conjuring and tricks are drama, and will interest some
  children. They take practice and need presentation skills.
  They are all about drawing an audience into believability.
  Check out your local library for books, or people who
  may have hidden talents who will demonstrate and teach
  children.
- Encourage comedians in your group, teaching delivery
  and punch line presentation. With help and confidence
  they may be able to write their own material, or use joke
  books as a starting point.
- Some children may be able to make simple puppets and

a puppet theatre for a short script on a topic suitable for a younger age group. When the drama is well rehearsed and ready, arrange for it to be presented. Interaction between groups fosters good relationships and is helpful to both younger and older children.

- Some children may be interested in learning camcorder skills. You may be able to find a mentor who can teach them. Let them learn and practise, filming a drama and showing the final edited version to the group.

- The same idea can be used for children who are interested in photography, make-up, PA, sound effects, etc. Make sure everyone has a role in the final production, and knows their value in its success.

- Write a simple action script based on your Bible or other story. Work out with children a musical interpretation of actions or feelings to accompany or replace spoken words e.g. use a three or five note sequence with different instruments representing anger, joy, fear, running, pain, jealousy, reconciliation, etc.

- Using well-known film theme CDs, challenge children to think of another storyline that would fit part of the film theme (e.g. *Star Wars, Attack of the Clones, Prince of Egypt*) and write a script for it to act out.

- Choose a well-known video. Turn down the sound and have characters act it out.

- Children can learn without any pain about people past and present as they prepare to interview someone famous. When the background work is done about the character, they can prepare a list of questions to be asked, and answers to be given. Video a variety of suitable TV interviews for children to watch so that they can learn interviewing skills that will draw out the drama of revelation.

EXAMPLE: KING JEHOSHAPHAT IN CRISIS

2 Chronicles 20:1–24, 29–30.
Create a TV interview with two of the men from Judah, when they returned to Jerusalem. What will the reporter ask them? How did you feel about the invasion? What did you think of King Jehoshaphat's idea of fasting and praying together? Did you join in? Did you believe it when the prophet said you wouldn't have to fight this battle? How did you feel as you set off for the desert? What had happened when you arrived? How do you think praying and praising God together helped?

• Choose a topic to be arranged as a radio phone-in or radio question time. Alternatively, a Bible character and his actions could be chosen as the topic. Children can pretend to be in a radio studio as presenter and audience. If children are not familiar with this format, listen to one together. They will need to invent and write out different people's funny or serious comments on the chosen topic and using different voices, phone the presenter, or be invited to give their comments/ questions from the audience. This can be recorded on tape and a studio set thought through and arranged. Children can listen to the phone-in afterwards. Intro and exit music can be added, and adverts.

• With your chosen story and simple script, discuss actions and movement. Using a white sheet, create a shadow play of your characters. You can also use this idea to shadow play hands, expressing emotions and feelings of the characters as the drama progresses.

- Choose a psalm e.g. Psalm 8, 29, and 65. Together, look at your chosen psalm in other versions of the Bible e.g. *The Message, God's Story*. Mark those parts of the psalm that have drama, action, emotion, character. Assign these to different children or small groups and ask them to create a sound for their part. Put these all together with expressive narration of the psalm.

- Build a psalm e.g. Psalm 93. One person begins with the first stanza and voices are gradually added stanza by stanza, until everyone completes the psalm together. Dance can also be effectively added to a psalm like this.

- Make up a TV news bulletin, with outside correspondents relating dramas from around the world.

In conclusion

You may mainly enjoy drama within the confines of your group, but a great deal of time and energy may have gone into your children's drama. Look for opportunities within the wider church and community to show their work e.g. all age services, school assemblies, local arts festivals, etc. Showing what you have produced to an audience is a whole new and helpful experience for many children, and very worthwhile.

11. Useful contacts

Kingdom Dance Resources
dance workshops, schools and children's groups, Family
Dance Days
www.kingdomdance.co.uk

Springs Dance Company
professional Christian Dance Company teaching in schools,
colleges, churches, theatres, missions, summer schools for
children and adults.
SpringsDC@aol.com

Christian Dance Fellowship of Britain
promotes dance and creativity as an expression of Christian
faith.
www.cdfb.org.uk

Crown Jewels
children's and Youth Dance group.
www.crownjewels.com

TranscenDance

a Christian Dance Company, communicating faith through dance with children and adults.

Lynne.Wright@ukgateway.net

Covenant players

provide thematic programmes through the medium of drama.

cpbio@compuserve.com

Riding Lights Theatre Company

productions and books: Lightning Sketches, Time to Act.

www.ridinglights.org

Viz a viz

drama and multimedia presentations.

www.vizaviz.com

Mimeistry

teaching and touring Christian Mime company.

www.mimeistry.com

Christians in Sport

www.Christiansinsport.org

Also available in this series:

Children's Ministry Guide to Dealing with Disruptive Children

by Andy Back

**A light, lively tone brings insight
to this tough subject. Compassion motivates
this volume, packed with practical ideas
as well as a helpful discussion of the
reasons behind disruptive behaviour**

1-84291-033-7

£4.99

Also available in this series:

Children's Ministry Guide to Tailored Teaching for 5-9s

by Sue Price

Evangelizing and discipling children requires an understanding of the way they think and develop. Easy-to-read insights into learning preferences and child development help you provide the best possible opportunity for each child to hear the good news and to grow in their faith.

1-84291-035-3

£4.99

Also available in this series:

Children's Ministry Guide to Storytelling

by Ruth Alliston

**Draws on the example of Jesus
as the master storyteller, and contains
a wide range of practical tips and ideas
for story styles and content. Makes your
storytelling more memorable for
the children in your care.**

1-84291-034-5

£4.99

Also available:

250 Songs
for Children's
Praise and Worship

Contains melody lines
plus lyrics and simple chords

complete with CD-ROM of all lyrics,
for use on overhead projectors
or with church song-projection software

ISBN 1–84291–065–5

£16.99

Also available:

Children's Ministry Teaching Programme

• age-appropriate teaching
in Leaders' Guides for
under 3s, 3-5s, 5-9s and 9-13s

• full colour activity sheets for
5-7s, 7-9s and 9-11s,
plus Y-Zone magazine for 11+

• craft ideas and resources for 3-9s

• resource CD with songs and stories

• FamilyZone magazine
with photocopiable words of songs,
pastoral and parents pages,
plus all-age worship service outlines

For free sample please call
01323 437749